2998

6

GONE ARE THE DAYS

GONE ARE THE DAYS

A New Horizons project by
the Senior Scribes.

Adrian Macdonald, Editor

Gall Publications,
Toronto, Canada

Center for Human Services,
New York, U.S.A.

First published 1975 by Gall Publications,
Box 6666-A, Toronto, M5W 1X4

ISBN: 88904   058   3

copyright © 1975
Gall Publications

Published simultaneously in the U.S.A.
by the Center for Human Services,
79 Madison Avenue,
New York, N.Y. 10016

Distributed by: SAANNES Publications Limited,
                   1293 Gerrard Street East,
                   Toronto, M4L 1Y8

Printed and bound in Canada

CONTENTS

THE SENIOR SCRIBES

Directors: Verna Adams
Helen Ball
Michael Foran
Kathleen Henderson
Adrian Macdonald
Dora Macdonald
Jean Suydam

Research Assistants: Kathy Healey
Karen Fawcett

General Assistant: Robert Skyvington

Financial Advisor: Patricia Reynolds

Treasurer: Michael Foran

Assistant Treasurer: Helen Ball

Artists: John Collins (J.C.)
Adrian Macdonald (A.M.)

Since this book was written, three directors
(Ralph Adams, Mary Martin, and Margaret
Wilton) have died. They were of invaluable
assistance to us in many ways.

The following people took part in discussion groups as part of the preparation of this book. Their assistance is very much appreciated.

Dr. Ralph Honey
Adrian Macdonald
Dora Macdonald
Mary Martin – deceased
Vincent J. McIntyre
Maurice H. Park – deceased

Several of the articles in this book have been prepared, not by an individual, but by a group. When this was the case, it was necessary to call on a ghost writer to pull the material together as a connected essay. Fortunately, we have a reasonably competent ghostly scribe haunting our eerie domain. But this spectre, who is rather shy, wished to remain unrecognized. We therefore gave him a pen name – Norman McPherson.

ABOUT THE AUTHORS

Helen Ball (born Toronto, 1897)

A writer of articles and short stories with three books of poetry published: "These Things Linger", "The Moment Snared" and "Person to Person".

Ethel Chapman (born Halton County, Ontario, 1900)

A lecturer with the Ontario Department of Agriculture for 25 years and associate editor of the "Farmer's Advocate" and the Winnipeg "Free Press Weekly". Her published writings include "God's Green Country", "The Homesteaders" and "With Flame of Freedom". She was awarded an Honorary Doctorate from the University of Guelph in 1963.

John H. Collins (born St. Catharines, Ontario, 1900)

With his degree in architecture, John assayed in Red Lake during the depression. He served with the Royal Canadian Engineers during the war and until his retirement was Director of Planning and Development for the Toronto General Hospital.

Michael Foran (born Wingham, Ontario, 1898)

Taught English for 22 years in various continuation and high schools, including De La Salle in Toronto. Retired from Massey Ferguson in 1964. Three books of poetry: "Night Flight", "This is my Worst" and "Twenty of my Best".

Kathleen Phillips Henderson (born Victoria Harbour,
Ontario, 1900)

Her long career includes working with the Registrar of
the Ontario Department of Education and the Managing
Director of S.S. Kresge Limited. She was closely in
touch with publishing through her husband, the editor
of Macmillan Company.

Adrian Macdonald (born St. Thomas, Ontario, 1889)

With his M.A. in English and Philosophy, Adrian taught
teachers how to teach for almost 40 years. He edited
"The School", and has published articles, short stories
and a book, "Canadian Portraits".

Dora Condell Macdonald (born Woodstock, Ontario, 1889)

Assistant to the editor of "Rod and Gun" for many years,
Dora was also society editor of the "Sentinel-Review".

Viola Pratt (born Atherley, Ontario, 1892)

Margaret H. Wilton (born Kingston, Ontario, 1903)

A graduate of Queen's University, for 30 years she was
in charge of the Technical Research Library in the
Ontario Department of Health. Two books of poetry have
been published: "Pageantry of Days" and "With the
Beauty of that Hour".

A GOLDEN AGE

The period which we are going to present (from 1895 to the outbreak of The First Great War) was one of the most fascinating in Canada's short history. It was a marvellous time to be alive, a time of fresh beginnings, a time when innovation and invention were in the air. During those years we saw many firsts, from the first horseless carriages (now motor cars) to the first wireless telegraph (now radio). The spirit of progress was everywhere present. The modern world was buoyantly emerging from the solemn Victorian era like a butterfly from a chrysalis.

In the early nineties most of those amenities, those conveniences which we take for granted today were lacking. Telephones were almost unknown. There was no electricity in the home or in the factory. There were no electric trolley cars or subway trains, only horse-drawn street cars. The streets were lit, none too adequately, by gas, and the homes by coaloil lamps. Cooking was done on a coal or wood range, and houses were heated by fireplaces or pot-bellied stoves. Few homes had indoor plumbing. Carpets were swept with a straw broom, after tea leaves had been scattered to lay the dust, and once a year they were taken up, a fearsome job, hung over a line in the backyard, and beaten with sticks or a carpet beater.

But by the time the period which we are going to picture was ended, all these amenities were commonplace. Everybody — well, almost everybody — had furnaces, telephones, electric lights, indoor plumbing, and phonographs. Motor cars were becoming common. To be sure, the early cars were cantankerous contraptions. In a later chapter one of our members will tell the story of an epic journey of sixty miles in an early automobile. But motoring became fairly reliable and moderately inexpensive with the introduction of the T—model Ford in 1908. And airplanes were not unknown. I have a photograph of an airplane which I took in the summer of 1910. In short, that brief period saw a complete transformation in the way of life of the people of Ontario. From primitive conditions that had not advanced much since pioneer days, the world for them had emerged into an era of sophistication and comfort.

It must be admitted, however, that all our marvelous discoveries were not so marvelous as we in our innocence supposed. Sometimes in our booming exuberance we mistook the dross for the gold, the shadow for the substance, the illusion for reality.

In 1899 Alfred Russel Wallace, who is given credit along with Darwin with having discovered the principle of natural selection in evolution, published a book entitled "The Wonderful Century". In it he dealt with all the wonderful discoveries made in the nineteenth century, and among the most extraordinary he cited phrenology. He described it as "a science of whose substantial truth and vast importance I have no more doubt than I have of the value and importance of any of the great intellectual advances already recorded". It is difficult for us today to imagine that phrenology was once regarded as an exact science. The theory that a person's abilities and traits of character can be determined by examining the contours of his head has been so completely discredited that we now regard the whole matter as a fraud or a joke.

Oh well! There are people even today who profess to believe in witchcraft or astrology.

In spite of our occasional follies, those were peaceful days, happy days. We knew nothing of the fear which lurks in a dark corner of our minds in these days of cold war, racial ferment, intercontinental ballistic missles, unrestrained violence,and spiritual disillusionment. Most of us were not rich, but there was plenty to do that did not require any great expenditure of cash. There were games of all sorts, amusing activities which we ourselves invented, roaming over the countryside on foot in summer or on snowshoes in winter, swimming in the lake or in some secluded nook of a river, reading books (most towns had excellent libraries) and dancing the waltz, the polka, or the two-step (not just spasmodic wiggling). Movies and vaudeville were cheap. It cost us only thirty cents or forty cents to take the girl friend out for an evening. Inflation was unknown. If we saved a dollar, it was worth a dollar when we came to spend it, not fifty cents, or thirty cents. And taxes, hidden or overt, did not grab most of what we earned.

A.M

Snowshoeing

It was an age free from the stultifying influence of over-organization and mass conformity. People could be people without having the rough edges rubbed off by the persistent hammering of television and radio, and the strident demands of fashion.

Those were the days when free enterprise really flourished. Big business had not gobbled up all the smaller businesses, as big fish eat the smaller fish in the ocean. At the turn of the century Beaverton, for instance, was just a village, but in it were a carriage works, which produced buggies and sleighs; a pottery; a creamery; a planing mill; a woollen mill, making blankets and other woollen goods; a foundry, turning out ploughshares, pumps, and other metal implements; a tannery; and a flour mill. Besides these industries there were the usual stores and services, all operated by their owners. Where are all these business enterprises today? Except for one or two, they have all been squeezed out of existence or absorbed by large corporations, many of them controlled by foreign capital.

In the years before the outbreak of the First World War we possessed a deep and abiding sense of security. We belonged to an Empire upon which the sun never set. Except for a few minor skirmishes, the peace of the world had been preserved for half a century by the might of Britain. Protected by the strongest fleet in the world, we were safe from aggression. Lesser breeds could not attack us — they would not dare. World peace, we fondly believed, was as firmly established as the Rock of Gibraltar.

This confidence in the British might was only made stronger by the South African War. At school we sang patriotic songs, like "The Soldiers of the Queen" and "The Maple Leaf Forever". We learned to hate the Boers because they hid behind rocks and shot down our brave soldiers with dum-dum bullets. And when Ladysmith was relieved, after a lengthy and determined siege, we celebrated the event with parading bands, impromptu speeches, and bonfires in the streets at night. The whole affair just proved to us how useless it was for anyone to resist the power of Britain.

The age when we were young was exuberant and assertive, sure of itself and pleased with life. We were the men and women of the new century, the great and glorious twentieth century. We were shaking off the inhibiting shackles of the past, and marching into the future with vision and courage. Nothing could stop us.

Some of our customers, it must be admitted, were quaint and amusing. The bathing suits which our prudery forced girls to wear are nowadays always good for a laugh. But it was a period that deserves more admiration than ridicule. There were no world wars, no carnage on the highways, no singing commercials, no thermonuclear bombs, no porno movies, no traffic jams, no rhythmic uproar passing itself off as music, no drug--induced sub-culture, no charismatic emotional orgy, posing as religious fervor, our lakes and rivers were still unpolluted, and young girls had too much sense to become hysterical over a group of male singers with flowing locks and voices like bereaved cows.

Is it any wonder that older people look back to it as a golden age, an age that we remember fondly, but an age that is gone forever. Our country will probably never see its like again.

EDWARDIAN ERA
by Michael Foran

The reign of King Edward was calm and serene;

It followed the age of the glorious queen.

With the world, so to speak, in the pink of condition —

No wars and no strikes, no nuclear fission,

No Stalin, no Hitler, no rash Mussolini —

The Kaiser was merely a harmless old meanie.

Then people were governed by strange inhibitions

Which now are considered outworn superstitions,

The lads of that era lived life to the full.

But, heavens, it must have been frightfully dull.

HOME LIFE IN THE MID-NINETIES
by Adrian Macdonald

In the mid-nineties of the last century a woman's place was in the home. The feminist movement was well under way in England and to a certain extent in the United States, but it had not as yet made its influence felt in the towns of Ontario. A married woman of the period would not think of going out to work. She stayed at home and looked after her husband and her children, and managed her house with great efficiency. She was the centre of the home, its guiding spirit, the rock upon which the home was founded. For this reason, if we wish to get the picture of the home life in 1895, we can't do better than follow a typical housewife through a typical day's activities. To make the contrast with life at the end of the period as striking as possible, let us take a typical day in mid-winter.

Jenny at the time that we have chosen was not yet thirty. She had three children, the oldest, Margaret, already in the First Book at school, and the youngest just under two years old. Her husband worked in a municipal office on the main street, a good fifteen minutes walk from home. His salary was less than a thousand dollars a year, which made it necessary for them to count their pennies. But they were not considered to be poor. Jenny had a maid to help her with the housework. In those days, when there were no electrical appliances, a maid was not a luxury for a woman with a family, but almost a necessity. And one could get a girl to live in the house (Thursday evenings off, if she had any place to go) for less money per month than one pays a cleaning woman to do six hours work today. What else was there for a girl to do?

Jenny's maid was called Rosie. She came from the country, and though she was willing enough, she was a bit slap-dash and clumsy.

On this particular morning Jenny opened her eyes one at a time, and very reluctantly, at ten minutes after seven. Her husband had already slipped out of bed without waking her. She could hear him downstairs shaking the fires and pouring fresh coal into the stove in the dining-room. The sound held an encouraging suggestion of life and warmth, as if blood were once more beginning to flow through the veins of the frozen household.

As Jenny's bare feet touched the cold floor, the framework of the house emitted a sharp crack like a pistol shot. The structural two-by-fours and the cross-beams, like the human inhabitants, were protesting at the bitter cold. Outside it was probably close to zero, and it was not much better in the bedroom. The only source of heat was the stove-pipe from the dining--room stove, which came up through the bedroom floor, and went across the ceiling to the chimney in the outside wall. But when the fire was banked down for the night the stove-pipe was almost cold.

Jenny could not see what it was like outside. The window was completely frosted over with an intricate pattern of frozen crystals. But it must have snowed over the night. When her husband had finished with the fires, she could hear him outside shovelling snow.

Jenny shoved her feet, which were blue with the cold, into a pair of carpet-slippers, pulled on a woolen dressing-gown over her flannelette night-gown, and turned to the cradle, where her youngest child was already awake and was watching her with round, inscrutable eyes. Without waiting to dress him completely, she bundled him in one of his small blankets, and sent him toddling towards the stairway. With the weather so cold she would wash both him and herself downstairs in the kitchen where it was warm.

The two older children and her father, who had lived with them since her mother's death, could stay in bed a bit longer.

In the morning Jenny looked rather a fright. Her hair was twisted up in curl papers and her dressing-gown was faded to a dusty blue. In the morning there was just no time to think of how she looked. She had to get things moving. Later in the day her beautiful dark brown hair would be coiled at the back of her head and teased into curls over her forehead. And her purple dress — though the styles of the period were the ugliest ever seen on women up to the time when they took to wearing trousers — was at least seemly and dignified.

When she got down to the kitchen she found that Rosie, the maid, had already shoved the kettle forward on the stove, and was busy setting the table for breakfast. Jenny's husband was shaving at the sink.

When he was dressed for church in his long Prince Albert coat and his tall silk hat, her husband looked, if not handsome, at least like a man who counted for something in the community. But like every other man he did not look his best when shaving. He wore only his heavy woolen underwear and his pants. His hair was rumpled, and half his face was still covered with lather, from which his moustache emerged like brushwood from a snowdrift.

Jenny lifted the cover off the porridge pot, and stirred the porridge vigorously. Left over night on the stove, it developed a crust that could be dispersed by stirring. Every morning except Sunday they had porridge for breakfast, oatmeal porridge with cream and brown sugar. They had brown sugar because it was cheaper than granulated sugar, 25 pounds for a dollar instead of 20. Sometimes Jenny's husband had an egg to follow the porridge.

On Sunday as a bit of a treat they had ham and eggs for breakfast. They needed extra sustenance on Sunday. It was the Lord's Day, a dismal day for everybody — no games, no secular music, no reading of anything but the Bible. In the morning they attended church, where they had to sit patiently through an hour-long sermon. Their minister was the Reverend J. A. Macdonald (he later became editor of the Toronto Globe) a burly Scot with a stammer. Often when he became deeply emotional in his sermon his jaw would lock open (an awesome spectacle!) and he would have to close it with his hand. After being properly edified by the service, Jenny and her family would return home to follow the extra-heavy breakfast by an extra--heavy dinner. Sunday in short was a day given up to the Glory of God and indigestion.

But we are following Jenny on an ordinary day, not Sunday. With breakfast over, her husband off to the office, and her oldest child off to school, Jenny and the maid were faced with the daily routine of chores. But before starting on the scheduled program, Jenny had a personal matter to attend to. She had to

Sunday

make a trip to the outhouse at the back of the yard. In winter this trip was anything but pleasant. Her husband had shovelled a narrow path from the back door, but her full skirt dragged in the snow on either side of the path, and wetted her stockings almost to her knees.

The unpleasantness of this trip for everybody, especially in mid-winter, undoubtedly caused wide-spread constipation. And the almost universal prevalence of constipation accounts for the great emphasis placed on the hygienic value of laxatives. One old doctor of the period gave as his prescription for a long and happy life, the admonition, "Fear God, and keep your bowels open." And Jenny's older sister, Mary, who had six children, lined them up every Friday night and gave them each a dessert-spoon of castor oil, whether they needed it or not.

As Jenny was returning from the outhouse she tried the pump over the well. As she feared, it was frozen. They had, of course, a pail of water in the kitchen, from which she kept the kettle full. But the pump would have to be freed before they could prepare dinner. She called to Rosie to bring the kettle of hot water, and the two of them struggled for twenty minutes before they got the pump to work freely.

To get the breakfast dishes out of the way quickly, they washed them together. The pump in the kitchen brought soft water from a cistern in the cellar. Then Rosie cleaned all the lamp chimneys and trimmed all the lamp wicks. Next she proceeded to make the beds. Meanwhile Jenny washed out a few of the youngster's duds that had been missed on Monday, scrubbing them clean on a washboard. There were, of course, no detergents either for the dishes or the clothes. But even in those days there were singing commercials. But people then were fortunate. The singing commercials were silent. On the wrapper of the soap was a picture of a choir singing lustily:

"A song we sing, a song of hope;
The world is using Comfort Soap."

When the washing was hung up round the kitchen to dry, Jenny put in an hour sewing.

In the house of the period the parlor was reserved strictly for company, and the dining-room which was usually quite large, was made to serve also as a general living-room. The sewing machine, which was operated by hand, (they could not yet afford the newer type operated by the foot) was kept in the dining--room. And most of the day Jenny's old father sat there with a shawl over his shoulders and a book on his knee.

"Father," said Jenny, before she started her sewing, "would you mind shovelling out the cellar steps? I want to bring up some preserves for pies."

"But my rheumatics is that bad —"

"A little exertion will make your blood circulate. I'm sure it will do you good."

"You're a hard woman, Jenny."

"Shovelling snow is no work for a woman. Now, wrap yourself up well, and you will come to no harm."

Continuing to grumble, the old man left the room.

Jenny was making a print dress for her oldest daughter, the one who was in school. It was going to be a very pretty dress, with embroidery at the collar and cuffs, and puffed-up sleeves just like a grown-up dress. Jenny was very clever with her hand--operated sewing machine. She made all her children's clothes and her own, and had even made a bathrobe and a smoking-jacket for her husband.

At half-past-ten she packed her sewing neatly in the sewing basket and returned to the kitchen to make pies. The first thing to do was to get preserves from the cellar to fill the pies. The entrance to the cellar was outside, a most inconvenient arrangement, which they were going to have changed as soon as they could afford it. But her father had finished shovelling out the steps, and she could get down to the cellar door without too much difficulty.

The housewife of the period did not buy cans of fruit from the store. She did her own preserving — whole fruit in a heavy syrup, jams and jellies, chillisauce, and pickles of all sorts. And apples were cut up and strung on strings to dry. From the rows and rows of jars, Jenny picked out two jars of peaches and two of raspberries. She was having company that evening, and she was making six pies.

When the pies were out of the oven it was time to get things ready for dinner, which was always served at noon. On this day it was to be beef stew. The meat had already been simmering on the stove for two or three hours. As she stirred the pot, she wondered if she had been skimpy with the meat. The butcher had asked 7 ¢ a pound for it, a scandalous price for stewing beef. She had thought of buying pork spareribs instead. They were only 2 ¢ a pound. But her husband did not like nibbling at what he called discarded bones. She helped Rosie cut up the onions and the carrots and peel the potatoes. When these were

A.M

Washday

safely in the pot, she had a few minutes to sit down and look at the newspaper, especially at the advertisements. Adam's dry--goods store was still advertising "the latest in dress materials in the most fashionable colors just in from Paris." She had not had a new dress for three years, and she decided that she would go down town that very afternoon and at least examine Adam's stock.

With dinner out of the way and the dishes washed, Jenny proceeded to make sandwiches for the forthcoming party. There would be eight people and in this cold weather everybody would be hungry. Furthermore all three children and their grandad would want their share before they went up to bed. She used the better part of two loaves of bread (a loaf of bread at that time was thirty-two ounces, not just twenty-four) most of a chicken, half a pound of cheese, and four hard-boiled eggs before she decided that she had made enough sandwiches.

She wrapped the sandwiches in damp dishtowels, and stowed them out of reach of the children on the pantry shelf.

The parlor, where the party was to be held, was a large room with a wall-to-wall carpet and an accumulation of furniture and

23

knick-knacks that would do credit to an antique shop today. The furniture was mostly made of walnut or rosewood, but there was little appreciation of the beauty of the wood. Walnut tables were covered with plush or velvet runners, and the rosewood piano was so heavily draped and so completely stacked with photographs and china ornaments that it was scarcely recognizable as a piano. Though the arms and legs of the chairs were elaborately carved, the backs and seats were constructed on the rightangle principle that made them acutely uncomfortable. Ornaments of one sort or another were displayed everywhere. There were wax flowers under a glass dome and a china Mandarin, who would nod his head if you moved him. There was an ornate lamp hanging from a hook in the ceiling. You pulled it up and down with a chain when you wanted to light it or blow it out. And about the room were two or three other lamps, one with an onyx base and a painted china bowl.

The room was always kept closed with the blinds drawn except when it was to be used for entertaining company. It smelled musty, like a second-hand book-shop, and was cold as a barn. Hours before the company was to arrive a fire had to be lit in the pot-bellied stove if the room was to be made warm enough for human habitation. Jenny's husband had laid the fire before he left for work. All Jenny had to do was light it, and when the kindling was going well, pour in coal from the fancy brass coal-scuttle.

The children had been surprisingly little trouble that morning. The youngest, a boy, had played with his blocks on the dining-room floor most of the morning. The second, a girl almost four, had gone to play with a friend across the road. The oldest was of course in school. But Jenny had an uncomfortable feeling, born of previous experiences, that as soon as she left the house to go shopping the two children who were home would raise a rumpus.

After dinner was eaten and the dishes cleared away, she wanted Rosie to sweep and dust the parlor, but she thought it best to have her first take the two children for a walk. She bundled the children up thoroughly, (a woolen muffler known as a cloud was wound around the throat and the lower part of the face) and watched the three leave the house. Then she herself got ready for her shopping trip.

If a woman of today were magically transported back eighty years to stand in Jenny's shoes (high buttoned shoes with low heels) on her front verandah that morning, she would be struck immediately, not only by the purity of the snow undefiled by city smog, but also by the utter silence. No whirr of motor-car tires on wet pavement, no roar of trucks mounting a slight incline, no scream of jets overhead. Just silence, broken only by the jingle of sleigh-bells and the occasional crunch of feet in the snow. There never has been any music quite like the jingle of sleigh-bells, a music that is heard today only in association with our blatantly commercialized Santa Claus.

The snow was piled high on either side of the path as Jenny made her way to the sidewalk, which earlier in the day had been cleared by a horse-drawn snowplow. It was a crisp cold day, but sunny. The shadows of the bare trees made intricate patterns on the glistening snow, and from every chimney along the street white smoke curled into the blue sky.

Usually at this time of day Jenny would meet one or other of her neighbors also bent on shopping. To a certain extent a shopping expedition was a social affair. But today the street was deserted.

Dr. Vanbuskirk in his red cutter, with a black buffalo robe over his knees, waved at her as he jingled past on some special call. As Jenny was wondering who could be having a baby or who was ill enough to require a doctor, the calm was shattered by the rapid clanging of a loud and insistent bell. Ding, ding, ding, rapidly — then a pause — followed by four strokes slowly. Once more the rapid clanging. And again the pause and the four slow strokes. It was the fire alarm, and the four slow strokes indicated that the fire was in Ward 4.

The doors of the fire-hall, which was a short distance ahead just short of the main street, were flung open and a team of horses appeared pulling the fire-engine. They were heavy draught horses, but in beautiful condition, sleek and shiny, with well-combed manes and flowing tails. As they turned towards Jenny they broke into a wild gallop. The hook-and-ladder truck followed.

Before you could shake a leg the whole street was alive with activity. Every door burst open. And people of every sort appeared on the sidewalk — old people and young people, scanti-ly-dressed people, and people muffled against the cold. Every-body in town responded to the tocsin of the fire-bell. The street, which a moment ago had been deserted, was now alive with people, some running after the fire-reels, and some chee-ring the firemen on, as the horses galloped furiously by. In tho-se peaceful days, a fire was the only exciting thing that ever happened.

Truth to tell it was an exhilarating spectacle — the galloping horses, the gleaming fire-engine belching smoke, and the fire-men with their large helmets.

For a moment Jenny felt an impulse to follow. But she re-strained herself. If she was going to do her shopping without being hurried she would have to be on her way. Then she re-membered Rosie and the children. She turned to see them dis-appearing up a side-street after the fire-reels. The two children were clinging to each other on a sleigh, and Rosie was running like a roebuck, pulling the sleigh with one hand and holding her skirts up almost to her knees with the other. Jenny laughed. But she made a mental note that she would have to speak to Rosie about exposing her legs in that unladylike manner.

The proprietor of the dry-goods store himself waited on Jen-ny. He was an apologetic little man, who looked at her over his spectacles, and caressed the bolts of material he was displaying with loving fingers. The price, 55 ¢ a yard, made her hesitate. But she knew that she had to have a new dress, and she finally settled on a navy blue soft silk, which she thought would be not only very dignified but extremely attractive. The proprietor measured out the material, and then the required length of brush. Brush was a coarse hairy material that was sewn inside the lower hem of the train to pick up the dust and protect the dress itself as it dragged along the floor.

When she got home Jenny found that Rosie and the children had not yet returned. This meant that she had to sweep and dust the parlor herself, and get the supper ready.

When she was just about to start dusting, however, she became aware of children's voices out in the backyard, shouting and laughing. The high-pitched tone of their hilarity was a sure sign that they were up to some devilment. Dropping her duster, she

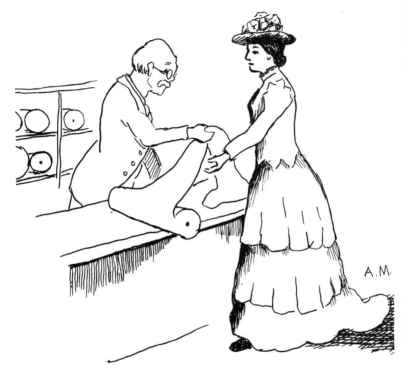

Shopping

went out to the back door. Her oldest daughter, Margaret, had got home from school, and was having an uproarious time with two boys from the neighborhood. Mrs. Hunt, a middle-aged widow who lived next door, always wore red knickers under her skirt in winter, and she had hung a pair of the knickers out on the line to dry. They were ballooned out by the wind and of course frozen stiff. And the three young tikes were making snowballs and tossing them over the fence into the distended undergarment.

"Margaret," Jenny cried indignantly, "What are you doing? "

"Nothing mummy. Just throwing snowballs."

"Stop it. Stop it immediately. What will Mrs. Hunt think? "

"It's nice clean snow, mummy."

"Come in here at once."

"Yes, mummy."

When she had scolded Margaret for her naughty behavior (Margaret was a young imp who was always in trouble) she went back to her dusting.

Rosie and the other two children came in at last covered with snow and brimming with excitement just as supper was ready. It had been a grand fire. A corner grocery store had been completely gutted, and all the contents, except a few things that the owner and the firemen had deposited in the snow, had been lost. Each of the children was grasping a large cucumber which he had picked up when a barrel of pickles had spilled in a snow--bank.

The party that evening was a great success. The company played progressive euchre with unrestrained gusto, and, when they were not laughing uproariously at some joke, they discussed the news of the day with shrewd solemnity. There were Albert Jenkins and his wife, who were neighbors. Albert had a pointed beard and was going bald, but he was quite a joker. His wife was a round-eyed dumpy little creature, dressed in a wine--colored cashmere frock with purple velvet vest inset and purple lace at the cuffs. Whenever her husband made one of his outrageous jokes she would look at him with adoring eyes and say, "Oh Albert! " There were Malcolm Murdoch and his wife, who were old friends. Malcolm was a huge man with a moustache like an unkempt hedge. He never saw the point of one of

Albert's jokes until he had pondered over it for three or four minutes, when he would suddenly burst out laughing. There was finally Fred Marshall, a second cousin of Jenny's and a confirmed bachelor; and Aunt Sarah, who always walked with a straight back as if she were on parade.

Through the evening, to be sure, there occurred one embarrassing incident. About ten o'clock in one of those moments when everyone is silent a plaintive old voice called down from the head of the stairs, "Jenny, Jenny. Where's the article?" Nobody laughed. Good manners forbade laughter. But everybody knew that the old man was looking for the chamber pot, which should have been under his bed.

Well after midnight Jenny and her husband went to bed. She slipped her dress, her chemise, and her woolen undervest off her shoulders, and donned her flannelette nightgown like a tent. Under its voluminous folds she removed her other clothing—her corsets, her two petticoats, her black woolen stockings, and her woolen underclothes. She prepared for bed in this highly complicated manner partly because of the cold, and partly from modesty.

One very proper matron of the period, who was the mother of thirteen children, boasted that never in her life had anybody, not even her husband, seen her without her clothes on; which assertion provoked a cynical member of a younger generation to remark that, considering all the circumstances, some awfully queer things must have gone on in the dark.

PIONEERS

He never owned a combine or a tractor;
He never saw a power-driven mower;
My father cut the grain with scythe and cradle
As men had done for centuries before.

He split the rails to build his wooden fences;
He walked uncounted miles behind the plow;
He drew the wheat to mill with team and wagon;
He pitched the hay by hand from load to mow.

My mother baked her bread and churned her butter;
She had no luxuries to buy or sell;
She made her yeast from hops, and soap from ashes;
She carried pails of water from a well.

She worked unceasingly from dawn to sunset
With patient hands that never seemed to tire,
She never turned a switch or pushed a button;
To make a cup of tea she built a fire.

And yet I wonder if this world we live in
Is better than the one that went before,
When men had never heard of atom bombing
Or constant threat of suicidal war.

Our parents lived their days as God intended
In sunlit valleys, close to birds and flowers;
In spite of all our vaunted march of science
Their quiet lives were happier than ours.

REVOLUTION ON THE FARM
by Michael Foran

"Let us not forget that the culti-
vation of the earth is the most
important labor of Man."

Daniel Webster

The latter half of the nineteenth century and the early years of the twentieth witnessed the most astounding changes in farming that had occurred in all the history of agriculture. Up to that time there had been no changes of importance since Biblical times. In the Bible there are many references to the reaping and binding of grain. We can picture Jesus walking through the hills and valleys of Palestine watching workers in the fields cutting grain with a sickle and binding it into sheaves exactly as they did 18 centuries later. Historians agree that the rapid modernization of farming methods in recent times was not so surprising as the fact that it was so slow in coming. All through the dark ages and through mediaeval times the farm laborers continued the back-breaking toil, cutting the grain, raking and binding, threshing with a flail, winnowing and sifting the chaff from the wheat. In 1807 Wordsworth wrote about the Solitary Reaper:

Behold her, single in the field,
Yon solitary Highland lass;
Reaping and singing by herself;
Stop here, or gently pass.

In Art, as in poetry, we have evidence of the same situation. Francois Millet painted his famous masterpieces, The Gleaners and The Angelus, to depict the age-old scene, the symbolic stoop of serfdom.

This lack of progress in farming is all the more amazing when we reflect that during all the centuries while no improvements were made in planting, reaping and harvesting grain, great progress was made in other fields. Great castles and churches were built, huge aqueducts brought water to the cities, Columbus discovered America, Magellan and Drake sailed around the world, weapons to destroy man (cannon and machine guns) proliferated, but no new farm implements appeared. Geniuses created great works of Art, composers produced immortal music, astronomers peered into the skies through wondrous telescopes, Gutenberg's printing press opened new fields in literature, but nothing was done to lighten the load of the lowly farmer who produced the most essential of all commodities — FOOD.

At last came the long awaited inventions. The sickle became a scythe, the scythe gave way to the cradle, the cradle was displaced by the reaper, and, at last came the binder. The binder, wonder of wonders, could cut the ripened wheat, bind it into sheaves, and deposit those sheaves on the fields in neat rows, ready to be hauled to the threshing machine. The revolution, after long centuries of waiting, had begun.

Following the successful introduction of reapers and binders there came a plethora of other inventions of labour saving devices to lighten the burden of the farmer. The horse rake, the horse-drawn mowing machines, along with gang plows, harrows, discs, seed drills, scufflers and cultivators soon became commonplace. These were all horse-drawn implements; it would still be many years before the gasoline engine was in common use. But in the era of which we are writing (viz 1895–1914) most of the above-mentioned implements were being produced in great quantities by a multitude of manufacturers. Fortunes were made by men like Cyrus McCormick who was one of the first of the tycoons who saw the need for agricultural machinery in the vast reaches of western United States and in the immense stretches of Canadian prairies, which were to become the bread baskets of the world.

But the machines did not lessen the unremitting toil of the average farmer. From early spring to late autumn the sons of the soil still worked from dawn to dusk.

Seeding time began as soon as the snow disappeared from the fence corners and when the fields which had been plowed in the previous fall were dry enough to cultivate. Farmers worked feverishly to get the grain planted as soon as possible because seed sown early would of course mature earlier and be of better quality.

Before sunrise each morning, the farmer ate breakfast hurriedly and finished the morning chores. He then harnessed the team, hitched them to the seed drill and started the tiresome task of tramping back and forth, back and forth, all day long, sowing the seed in straight even lines, watching the wheelmarks of the previous round to be sure he did not skip or overlap on the sown land. He also watched the hopper of the drill to see that the grain was running properly down through the hose. When the hopper needed refilling he replenished it from one of the bags of grain at the side of the field. An average farm in those days consisted of 100 acres, of which perhaps 40 acres was in grain. The "seeding", therefore, might take two or three weeks.

One project led to another. The cattle were let out "on the grass" early in May. Seeding would be finished about the same time. A late spring would throw the timetable all out of kilter.

Mid-June saw the start of the heaviest work of the year — haying. On my father's farm the haying operations occupied three or four weeks, depending on the weather and the number of acres in hay. The work was done in four stages — cutting, raking, "coiling" and "drawing in". Clover, alfalfa and timothy hay ripened at different times. I've heard my father say "Clover's fit to cut, we'll start hayin' tomorrow." Next day he harnessed the heavy team of horses and started mowing. He had a six-foot-cut mower and by nightfall several acres were lying in neat swaths. Then if all went well he started the alfalfa. My job commenced next day. As a little gaffer about ten years old I was given the task of hitching the old mare to the horse rake and raking the clover while dad was cutting alfalfa.

Old time buildings

I rather enjoyed this phase of the work. Back and forth all day long I would direct the operation like an expert engineer, dumping the rake at proper intervals, leaving the hay in neat straight windrows, ready for the men who came with their pitchforks to pile it up in small stacks which we called coils. By the time the timothy was cut and coiled we could start drawing in the red clover. It took several days for the hay to be "cured" properly, ready for storing in the big mow in the barn.

"Drawing in" was hard work. The big wagon rack was set in place on the wagon bolsters, the heavy Clydesdale horses were hitched up, and the wagon was driven through the gap which had been opened in the rail fence into the clover field. One man drove the team and built the load, the other pitched on, a back-breaking job. The owner of the farm usually drove the team and built the load, while the hired man, walking beside the wagon, pitched up coil after coil till the wagon was groaning and creaking under the weight. Then the farmer clicked to the horses, and headed for the barn. The big strong horses leaned forward, straining every muscle, and the wagon wheels creaked as if protesting the heavy load. At the barn it required a supreme effort to drag the load up the slope and on to the barn floor.

Then came the farmer's heaviest task. He had to pitch the hay by hand from the load up into the mow, where the hired man threw it back, levelling it into the corners.

About the turn of the century the more affluent farmers could afford a hayloader, that strange-looking contraption drawn behind the wagon. It would pick up the hay from the windrow and transport it by a series of chain-driven carriers up to the man who was building the load. Moreover, a new method of lifting the hay into the mow from the wagon was introduced on some farms in the early days of the 20th century. A huge steel fork was attached to a "car" which ran on a wooden track fastened to the roof of the barn. This hayfork, about six feet long, was driven down into the hay on top of the load. A long thick rope led from the car down to the barn floor where it was tied to the whiffle-trees behind the horses. The horses were driven down the gangway and the great "lift" of hay was drawn up into the mow. Three or four "lifts" would take all the hay from the wagon.

Harvesting in the nineties

These labour saving devices helped a great deal to lighten the burden of haying, but many farmers could not afford the expense of buying hayloaders and hayforks. For them the fearful toil of haying is best expressed in a bit of verse written by one of my favorite poets. It is called "Farmers' Hay-day".

These are the days when the farmers are verily
    earning their bread by the sweat of their brow,
Facing the blistering sun in the hayfield
    or choking with dust in the heat of the mow;
Feeding the world, while the city-bred parasites
    loaf in an office or loiter at ease,
Bosses of Unions and all of their minions
    are fed through the labour of toilers like these.

But we must not forget the part played by the farmer's wife
in this busy season. The farmer's hardest work is done in the
heat of summer when city slickers take their holidays. As a result relatives and friends choose that time to visit their hard-
-working country cousins. City folks love the open air and the
sumptuous meals provided by the farmer's wife. Again I may
be allowed to quote the poet to describe the antics of the visitors. It runs thus:

Oft in the kitchen they talk to the housewife
    while greedily wolfing her muffins and pies,
Telling her stories of golfing and fishing,
    and most of their tales are preposterous lies,
Pompously boasting of places they've visited —
    Boston, Muskoka, Chicago, New York,
But never a foot do they put in a haymow,
    never a hand do they lay on a fork.
The overworked woman, distraught and perspiring,
    is told that she lives in perpetual bliss,
And her husband, returning from back-breaking labor,
    is greeted with asinine speeches like this:

    "Oh, what a joy is a country vacation;
    Weather so clear and delightfully hot;
    Farming is just an ideal occupation. "

    God! It's a wonder they never get shot!

I should mention here that there was one job during the haying season that I actually enjoyed. That was "minding the gap".
When I was a mere stripling seven or eight years old, too young
to do the heavy work, my job was to keep the cattle from wandering into the hayfield. The gap, as we called it, was an opening in the rail fence through which the loads of hay were drawn

to the barn. I was on guard there to keep the cows from wandering from the pasture field into the hayfield. While I was on duty, there was no need to open and close the gap every time the wagon went through. I had a good deal of time to myself so I had a chance to manufacture bows and arrows, darts, and even windmills. At one time I had four windmills mounted on fence posts, clattering away day and night when a strong wind was blowing. Once, I remember, my brother showed me how to make a willow whistle. It was a thrill to cut the small branch, about six inches long and an inch thick, slide the bark off, put in the proper notches, replace the bark, and hear the clear notes of the whistle, my very own.

I wonder if there are many lads today who could amuse themselves as I did, making wooden windmills, fighting imaginary enemies hidden in clumps of bushes near the gap. I would attack one of these bushes fiercely, shooting arrows at red Indians. We had an old stump fence beyond the crooked rail fence where there was a cluster of stumps resembling a castle. I thought of myself as a Greek soldier, defending the castle against the Persians, warning King Leonidas that the Persians had so many troops against us that their arrows darkened the sun. Then, replying for Leonidas, I would shout, "So much the better, we shall fight in the shade."

At last when the haying season was over, harvesting began. By the time I was in my teens my father had purchased a Massey--Harris Binder, a marvellous machine. Drawing it out of the driving-shed where it had been stored all winter, we oiled it completely, every cog-wheel and roller, put on the three canvasses, and drew it into the wheat field. The needle had to be threaded, with the twine carefully drawn from the twine-box to the knotter. Then with two or three horses straining in their harness, the operation of harvesting began. The rolling reels whipped the grain back onto the table canvas, which carried it to the deck canvas. Up and over the deck went the loose grain, down into the packers where the big needle wrapped the twine around it and the knotter tied it in a tight sheaf. The kickers kicked the sheaf out onto a sheaf carrier. The farmer, with a motion of his foot, could trip the sheaf carrier, depositing several sheaves neatly bound, ready for the hired man who followed, stooking the wheat. A good man could stook the grain almost as fast as it was cut. We had come a long way from the time when the cutting was done by a sickle.

This "drawin' in" would take two or three weeks. Day after day, back and forth, loads from the front field, from the middle field, from the corner field and the back field were drawn into the barn and mowed carefully in the big mow. If the barn was not big enough to hold all the sheaves we often had to build a stack close to the big doors where the separator would be placed when threshing time came.

To a tiny country urchin threshing was an exciting event. The three units of the equipment consisted of the steam-powered traction engine, the water tank built onto a heavy wagon, and the huge grain separator. I can recall with vivid memory the sight of that procession moving slowly down the sideroad, heading for Foran's farm. I would rush into the kitchen and shout "Momma, the "trashin' outfit is here." My mother would be busy manufacturing scads of apple pies and cakes and cookies to be devoured by the threshers next day. Dad would be in the barn cleaning the thresh floor and making last minute preparations for the great event. I would watch every move as the big engine, puffing and blowing, would swing slowly into Foran's gate, drawing the huge separator behind. I envied the man driving the steaming monster and adjusting the throttle as he turned. His assistant, driving the water tank, brought up the rear.

Word spread quickly through the neighborhood that the threshing machine had come. Sometimes there was a controversy regarding who would be threshed first, but usually the "machine" just went up one concession and down the next.

The actual threshing was a big undertaking, not only for the men involved, but for the weary housewife who had to prepare the food. Usually there were at least twelve men in the gang. There was the engineer, the separator man, the tank man, four or five in the mow, and at least two carrying boxes. These were round steel boxes, or baskets, in which the grain was carried from the separator to the granary. They were placed at a spout near the middle of the machine, where the golden grain, newly threshed, flowed out in a thick stream. When the "box" was full the man on the job picked it up, put another in its place, and hurried to the granary where he dumped the box into a bin, and hurried back to the separator to repeat the procedure. If the oats or barley was a good crop the grain would roll out the spout faster than one man could handle it, and two men were needed. Usually there was a wooden tally board in the granary with pegs in holes. When a "box" was emptied into the bin a peg was moved on the board from one hole to the next, thus keeping count on the number of bushels poured into the bins.

I believe the worst job in the threshing was performed by the men in the mow. All day long they forked the sheaves forward from one to another, bringing them to the front where a man known as the feeder threw them into the roaring maw of the machine. Down in there somehow the grain fell into the spout leading to the bushel boxes mentioned above. The straw went back to the "blower", a long pipe projecting out into the barn-yard where the strawstack grew steadily until it became a huge pile of yellow fodder, to be used for feed or bedding in the long winter months ahead.

The first time I was ever asked to do a man's work at the threshing was when I was about 15 years old. I was attending high school in a town 12 miles from home. I rode back and forth on a bicycle. On a certain Saturday I arrived home on my bicycle to learn that one of the men had taken ill and I had to take his place in the mow. I dreaded the job. But I found a pitchfork and bravely climbed up the ladder into the mow where the operation was in full swing. Four or five men were steadily forking the sheaves toward the machine. They were tough, hard-muscled, sturdy farmers to whom this was just another day's work. The dust was dense. It got into one's eyes, ears, nose and mouth. When meal time came the men climbed down the ladder and headed for the farm house. Without washing, they sat down at the table. Streaks of perspiration and dust lined their cheeks. They ate hurriedly and ravenously. In half an hour they were out having a few minutes to smoke their pipes or talk about the yield before they climbed once more into the mow. The big engine started, the long belt flopped hesitantly, then the whole machine roared into life.

Eventually, the threshing season was finished. In two or three weeks every farmer up and down the concession was "threshed out". My father, of course, helped at all the threshings of neighbors who, in turn, had helped him. It was customary at other times, too, such as in haying or harvesting to help one's neighbors. No money was involved.

The end of the threshing season, of course, did not mean that the farmers could relax. They never took holidays. There was corn to be cut and stooked, apples to be picked and stored in bins in the cellar, roots had to be put in the root house, and finally there was the fall plowing to be done. Every good farmer wanted to get his land plowed in the fall; spring plowing was not as good as fall plowing. All through October and November (and often into December if we had a late fall) the farmer hitched the team to the plow and plowed the fields which were to be sown next spring. Different crops required different kinds of plowing. There were disc plows, twin plows, gang plows and narrow plows. All through the long autumn days the plowing continued until the first heavy snowstorm put an end to it. Archibald Lampman, one of our best poets of the late 19th century, wrote a poem entitled "In November" which describes the scene in a farmer's field during the first snowfall. It ends thus:

"The woodmen's carts go by me homeward-wheeled
Past the thin fading stubbles, half concealed,
Now golden-gray, sowed softly through with snow,
Where the last plowman follows still his row,
Turning black furrows through the whitening field."

Even in mid-winter there was no respite for a farmer. After a heavy snowstorm or blizzard, when snow piled up four or five feet deep on the concessions, the roads had to be kept open. They called it "breaking the roads". The heaviest horses would be harnessed, hitched to the sleigh, and driven out into the white, trackless expanse. Up and down the lane several times, they tramped, then out on to the sideroad, plunging through the drifts, belly-deep in mounds of snow. Other farmers did the same, and eventually the concessions and sideroads would be passable once more. The sleigh-bells attached to the harness made merry music as the horses trotted home. Parts of the road, swept bare by the wind, would be covered with ice. Farmers, wise in the ways of winter, took their teams to the nearest blacksmith to have them "sharp-shod". The flat shoes used in summer work were replaced with sharp-corked ones. Horses

welcomed this operation. They realized that with the sharp-
-corked shoes they could travel over icy surfaces without danger
of falling.

There was also the problem of keeping a huge supply of fire-
wood in the woodshed to keep the big kitchen range roaring
on cold winter nights. This meant breaking the road down the
lane to the bush. The sleigh was loaded in the bush, drawn up
the lane to the house and unloaded into the woodshed, to be
piled and split ready for the woodbox beside the kitchen stove.

In the bush we cut a supply for the following year. We select-
ed trees to be felled, notched them with an axe, cut them
through with a cross-cut saw, and dropped them, if possible,
in an open area. Often they would lodge in another tree as they
came down, so the other tree would have to be cut down also.
Then we trimmed off the branches, cut the trunk into blocks
about 18 inches long, and split the blocks into slabs. The slabs
were piled in convenient places and left to dry out for use the
following winter. The dry slabs a year old would burn much
better than green wood freshly cut.

In addition to these activities there were always the winter
chores to keep us busy. Twice a day cows had to be milked.
I remember an old farmer saying. "No matter what you say
about the busy, hardworking farmer's life, there's one thing
sure; it's the cows that keep my nose to the grindstone. Twice
a day, seven days a week, them consarned cows have to be milked. You can skip almost every job for a day or two except the
milkin'. Even on a quiet Sunday in winter, you gotta milk them
cows. If you go out to a friend's place for an evening meal, you
gotta get home to the milkin', come hell or high water."

Of course that wasn't all the "chores". You had to separate
the cream in the old De Laval separator. Then you had to feed
the calves, feed the cattle, feed the horses, hens and pigs, clean
the stables and put fresh straw in the stalls for beddin'. Only
then could you trudge back to the farmhouse, happy in the
knowledge that the animals were warm and comfortable, and
able to snooze safely through the long winter night.

But there were pleasant evenings too, events that relieved the
monotony of the long winters. Often there were dances at the
little red schoolhouse, or in the hall below the church. There

were also frequent card parties with fiercely contested games of euchre or "500". When a euchre player held all the high cards with the right and left bowers he pounded the table vigorously and shouted in glee when he won a "lone hand". The coal-oil lamp bounced on the table when winning hands were slapped down.

Country dances were especially enjoyable. The milking and other chores would be done early in the evening, horses would be hitched and harnessed to the big sleigh, the family would be wrapped in Buffalo robes and the sleigh bells would sound merrily on the way to the "party". There was always someone among the neighbors who could play the fiddle, and one of the girls who could "chord" on the old organ. Late into the night, or early morn, the sound of music and song resounded through the frost-chilled countryside.

Occasionally there were barn dances. These were of course on a larger scale than the house parties. Usually they occurred in the early summer before the hay and grain were stored in the barn. Often they were held to celebrate a barn raising. A new barn was a fine place to celebrate. The "thresh floor" of the barn was perhaps 40 feet in length and 25 feet across, so there was room for at least ten "sets" of square dancers. Most of the dances were "squares". The man who "called off" would sing out the changes to the old familiar tunes of "Turkey in the Straw", the "Irish Washerwoman" and similar unforgettable melodies. "Alleman left" and "do-si-do on the corners all". Few of the dancers knew the meaning of those old expressions.

As the night progressed the excitement and the noise increased. Many of the men would have bottles of whisky to cheer them up. (It was only a dollar a quart in those days.) Sometimes the barn dances would last till almost morning. That reminds me of a story about my own mother. She scolded me when I had grown up, about twenty years later, for staying out too late at parties. But I reminded her of a story of a barn dance which she had told me. When she herself was a teen-ager she was at a merry dance where the lads tried to conceal the fact that there was a brightening of the sky in the east, indicating that the sun would soon be shining. So they hung a horse blanket over the window in the east end of the barn, thereby prolonging the merriment until after the sun had actually risen.

The demure young ladies were shocked to discover that they had to drive home in broad daylight.

We must admit that any pleasures those brave people got from their square dances, card-playing and such shenanigans were richly deserved. It was a life of toil, unceasing toil, for both men and women. The men were hard-living, hard-drinking, hard-working, but for the most part, honest, decent citizens. Their women were equally dedicated and indefatigable. Most of the women were mothers of large families, carrying on with their myriad duties without a word of complaint. Modern women, especially those of the Women's Lib temperament, would hold up their hands in horror at the prospect of living in such an environment.

SCHOOL DAYS

by Norman McPherson

In the old school which I attended as a boy the day opened in the upper grades with Bible reading and a prayer. And by George! we needed the prayer. The next item on the program was mechanical arithmetic — addition, subtraction, multiplication, and division. On the blackboard were written an addition question as long and wide as a strip of wallpaper, and three other sums equally formidable. When the allotted time was up we exchanged scribblers and marked the answers right or wrong. Woe to those who made too many errors! They would have to stay in after four, and do another set of sums.

The main purpose of teaching arithmetic in those days was to produce ready reckoners. I once knew a man who could add a three-digit column as readily as I could add a single-digit column. But today things are very different. Cash registers, electronic calculators, and computers now do most of our calculating. All that is left for most of us is to figure out our income tax, or total up a bridge score. Modern courses in mathematics no longer concentrate on training ready reckoners, but instead aim at developing creative and imaginative mathematical minds.

To keep my mind alert and up to the minute (I've been a bit worried about my brain lately) I have put a good deal of study on the new mathematics, and I think that I have got the hang of it.

Here is a simple contemporary problem. In the supermarket oranges are priced at 6 for 49c, but you want to buy only 4. How much would you have to pay?

Let us approach the problem in the proper creative and imaginative manner. It is easier to understand the operation that must be performed (Lord knows why, but so the book says) if we use expanded notation; so, since none of us is any too bright, that's what we will do. The price of the oranges is therefore (6 x 1) oranges at (4 x 10) (9 x 1) cents.

Now, it is obvious that we are dealing with three sets of oranges: the set of all the oranges in the store, the set of 6 oranges which is priced at 49c, and the set of 4 oranges which is in our basket. We may represent these sets respectively as A, B, and C. The first set is a universal set, which we may denote by the numerals (1, 2, 3, 4, 5...) in brackets. The three dots suggest that the set is extended indefinitely. Set B we may represent as (1, 2, 3, 4, 5, 6). And set C as (1, 2, 3, 4). The last numeral in B, as in C, represents the number of oranges in the set. If we compare the three sets point-to-point we will see that set B is a subset of set A, and that set C is a subset of set B.

Now that we see clearly what our problem is (at least, I hope we do) we can proceed with the appropriate algorithm. An algorithm is a convenient procedure for finding the result of an operation on two numbers when the result is not immediately apparent. The two numbers we are first concerned with are 6 and 49, both of which for easier manipulation we write in expanded notation — (6 x 1) and (4 x 10) (9 x 1). It is suggested that for the forthcoming operation the numbers be arranged, not in vertical array, but in horizontal disarray.

Division is the most difficult of the algorithms, involving as it does...

Oh hell! The price of the four oranges is 33c (32 2/3c to be exact) so why not pay up and be done with the whole matter.

Mathematics has supplanted Latin in schools today as the mystic discipline which everyone must study, why God only knows! I don't.

* * *

Grammar in our day was almost as gruelling an ordeal as arithmetic. We really studied English grammar. Or was it Latin grammar imposed on English? We spent hours parsing and analysing. Often our study of grammar provoked hot discussions in the class. One boy "compared" ill by writing "ill, sick, dead", and we argued for half an hour as to whether that were not just as correct as saying "ill, more ill, most ill".

Whether this intensive study of grammar induced us to speak correctly is open to question. But it at least gave us a vocabulary for discussing good usage. Ever afterwards we knew what was meant when somebody said, "But, my dear sir, your participle is dangling." Or, "Do you think it wise, sir, to, without rhyme or reason and for no good purpose, split an infinitive — — or, in fact, any verb form? "

In school today pupils no longer study English grammar. They just putter with it. The result is that English usage is determined by the illiterate. In schools, youngsters are taught that it is wrong to say, "What is that sausage made of? " because some pedantic ignoramus once declared that it is wrong to end a sentence with a preposition. But they are not taught that it is incorrect to say, "Divide that sausage between you and I." And that, my love, is just as bad as saying, "Give the whole damned sausage to I."

A preposition takes the objective case of the pronoun — simple, isn't it?

Would it not be better to drop the humbug of pretending to teach English grammar, and instead to develop a course in English usage? Grammatical concepts could be introduced just enough to explain cases where grammatical principles determine correct usage.

* * *

Our history textbook was very British, and thoroughly jingoistic. Apparently we were the only really good people, and we had licked almost everybody. Undoubtedly much of the ill will among nations today is caused by the distorted view of history given in school textbooks. It would be interesting to compare the account of the war of 1812 in an American textbook, with that in a Canadian textbook. What a marvellous thing it would be if the history textbooks of Quebec, and the history textbooks of the rest of Canada could be brought closer together.

We laugh at the fervid patriotism of those old textbooks. But they had one good effect. They turned out a generation of young people who were intensely Canadian. In the late eighties of last century, a great many liberals, both in Quebec and in English-speaking Canada, were openly in favor of annexation by the United States. They were attracted by extremely generous terms offered by President Harrison. But our generation would have regarded such sentiments as disloyal, almost traitorous. We were Canadians, proud of ourselves and immensely proud of our vast country.

* * *

Geography was studied apart from history, not just as one element in that conglomerate stew now called social studies, which is a bit of everything and not much of anything. We really studied geography, committing all sorts of things to memory — the counties and county towns of Ontario, the states of the United States and their capitals, the exports and imports of many foreign countries, and the boundaries of Canada, the United States, and of most European countries. Boundaries seemed to be of paramount importance. We had to remember every little river, every unimportant strait, every parallel of latitude. In the early days of World War One we were deeply disturbed by the ease with which the Germans overran boundaries which we had so painstakingly memorized.

* * *

Young people may sometimes wonder why men and women of our generation have such mournful faces. They probably assume that it is our rheumatism that is troubling us, or that we are sad because we are no longer young. But they would be wrong. We are perfectly contented to be old, and when you are past seventy you take a bit of arthritis and the other ills this flesh is heir to just as something you must put up with.

No. Our sad expression is due, as psychologists will no doubt have guessed, to a traumatic experience in early childhood. We are sad because of the effect on our tender young minds of having to live for two full years with that old "Third Reader", the Dismal Reader.

It began with the story of the "White Ship", which crashed on the rocks when crossing the channel from France to England, and was lost. On it were the king's son, his sister, the king's niece, her brother, and three hundred other poor souls, most of them gentlefolk. Only one man was saved, a poor butcher from Rouen. When the king was told of the tragedy, he "fell to the ground like a dead man, and never, never afterwards was seen to smile". This mournful yarn was followed by the pathetic story of Lucy Gray, who lost her way in a snowstorm, and, when trying to cross a narrow bridge, fell into the river and was drowned. (No, she was not staggering home from a cocktail party.)

Lucy Grey   A.M.

Then came the tale of the "Poor Little Match Girl" who, on a cold and snowy New Year's Eve had "walked along the street with naked feet, benumbed with cold, and carrying in her hand a bundle of matches, which she had been trying all day to sell, but in vain; no one had given her a single penny." Next morning she was found frozen to death, with a bundle of burnt matches by her side. She had lit one match after another to keep her fingers warm. That was followed by a poem that told how Mary had been sent to call the cattle home across the sands O'Dee, but, though she had lived by the sea all her life, she forgot about the tide. And — yes, you've guessed it. Her body was found next morning floating among the nets by fishermen.

A pathetic poem which was attuned to the Victorian era, but not to modern times was "The Old Arm Chair". It fairly drips with sentimentality, and sentimentality is no longer in fashion.

"I love it, I love it, and who shall dare,
To chide me for loving that old arm chair?
I've treasured it long as a sainted prize.
I've bedewed it with tears, and embalmed it with sighs."

Why all the sighs and tears? "A mother sat there." And of course the old girl is now dead.

Such fulsome sentimentality would make the young people of today feel nauseated. In their reading they much prefer sex to sentiment, and violence to filial devotion.

Much more in keeping with the feeling of today was Dickens' story, "Prince Arthur". It began, "At two-and-thirty years of age, in the year 1199, John became king of England. His pretty little nephew Arthur had the best claim to the throne." In those two sentences you have the making of high tragedy. John, who was a very evil man, had his nephew thrown into prison. And not content with that dastardly deed, sent certain ruffians "to blind the boy with red-hot irons," a really low down trick even for those days. But Hubert de Bourg, noble man, who was warden of the castle in which the boy was imprisoned, refused to let the ruffians enter. To get rid of the boy John was forced in the end to resort to a more devious scheme. One dark night the boy was stabbed. His body was sunk in a river with heavy stones, and "never more was any trace of the poor boy beheld by mortal eyes."

We didn't, of course, feel so badly about Ralph the Rover, who was a pirate. He got what was coming to him. Just for devilment he had cut down a bell which the pious Abbot of Aberbrothock (can you pronounce that name? We could) had placed on the Inchcape Rock. And some time later in a wild storm his own ship was wrecked on this very rock.

"But, even in his dying fear,
One dreadful sound could the Rover hear,
A sound as if, with the Inchcape Bell,
The fiends below were ringing his knell."

And so it went on, from "The Wreck of the Hesperus" to the "Burial of Sir John Moore" until we came to the most pathetic of them all, "The May Queen". When the noble Alfred set out to do a bit of tear-jerking, he could do it with a master's hand. To make the gloom last as long as possible, the pathetic story was not given to us in a single bitter dose, but was divided into three sections, called First Reading, Second Reading, and Third Reading. (Sounds like a bill in parliament, doesn't it?) In the first section the young minx who is the subject of the poem wants to be called early, because she is to be May Queen. But not long after that frolic is over and done with she develops what used to be called "galloping consumption", or something of the sort. By New Year's Eve she knows she will soon die, but she still wants her mother to call her early (why in hell she didn't buy an alarm clock, I never understood) because it will be the last New Year she will ever see. And sure enough on a wild March morning she kicked the bucket.

In fairness it must be admitted that the old Third Reader contained some extracts that were not doleful. The book ended with the merry tale of John Gilpin, who clung unwillingly to the back of a run-away horse, much to the amusement of all who saw him. There were also improving articles of an informative character. We learned all about the giraffe, which strange to relate, has no voice; the hippopotamus, which of all the ugliest-looking animals is certainly the ugliest; the crocodile, which is sly and wary; and many other interesting creatures. In fact, though it contained only 280 pages and cost only thirty cents, the book was a treasure house, not only of mournful dirges, but of general information.

Each of the readers served us for two years, and there is no doubt that we were thoroughly familiar with the contents, especially the poetry, when at long last we passed on to the next book. We studied each selection thoroughly, we wrote out the meanings of the unfamiliar words and phrases, we learned to spell the hard words, we used certain sentences for grammatical analysis, and we read the selection aloud over and over again. The language of the poems was woven into the very fabric of our minds; and the imagery colored our outlook on life. Long years afterwards many of us can repeat by heart most of the poetry we studied in school.

Two poems especially seem to have impressed our young minds, one in the Third Reader and one in the Fourth. If you start anyone over seventy with the lines —

"By Nebo's lonely mountain,
On this side Jordan's wave,
In a vale in the land of Moab..."

he will probably go on to the end of "The Burial of Moses" unless you hit him over the head with a club. And Gray's "Elegy Written in a Country Churchyard" is graven on our memories as firmly as the legends on a tombstone.

The children of today are subjected to an even more intensive poetic conditioning, but not in school. It is not the teacher, but radio and television that now do the job. What a storehouse of beautiful memories these children will have when they get to be seventy — a multiplicity of jingles about toothpaste, laxatives, and detergents! When they sit around a radiant heater on some cold winter evening and warm their hearts with instant whisky (empty contents into glass of water and stir) they will still be wondering where the yellow went and expressing in song their undying love for chewing gum and downy bathroom tissue. Add to this conditioning, the effect on young minds of the appalling bathos that characterizes the lyrics of popular songs, and you will understand why a taste for poetry is nonexistent today.

Our memory of the primary grades is not so clear as our memory of the upper grades. By the way, the term grades was not used in our day. We referred to ourselves as being in the second book, junior or senior; or the fourth book, junior or senior. When I started to school in the mid-nineties we were taught to recognize words in our readers by spelling them. That is why I am such an expert speller today. I can spell words like hipoppotumus three different ways in one paragraph, and even Shakespeare could not do better than that.

The introduction of phonics in the teaching of reading was looked on as a marvelous step forward. At first in teaching by the phonic method, each letter sound was introduced separately and was provided with an association to help the memory. S was a serpent, and serpents hiss; M was three beehives placed side by side and bees hum. This method improved on the spelling method, but was still slow. Today the letter sounds are presented in "meaningful" settings and the reading material is interesting and plentiful. If the modern method is employed skillfully, most of the pupils develop into highly competent readers.

* * *

Recently I heard an enthusiastic young school teacher, inspired by the results of the Hall—Dennis Report, declaring that at last schools are being made attractive to children, that today children really enjoy going to school. Did we hate school sixty or seventy years ago? Not a bit of it. We enjoyed school just as do youngsters today. To be sure we were taught a good deal of tiresome and useless rubbish; to be sure there was far too much emphasis on rote memory, far too little on creative activity; to be sure the walls between classes had not been knocked down so that our roving minds could be free and unconfined; to be sure the discipline was much stricter than today. But youngsters have a built-in defensive mechanism which closes off their minds when they are bored, and preserves their intense interest for periods when they are not dominated by adults. Undoubtedly things are better today. But if a bit of the old-fashioned school's regular routine, and much more of its firm but kindly discipline were reconstituted in our present schools, children would not be dropping out because they are confused, and the drug traffic among pupils could be licked in a fortnight.

A RURAL WOMEN'S MOVEMENT

by Ethel Chapman

In the period of our concern, the years 1895 to 1914, a movement had its beginning in Ontario that has since spread to every province in Canada and to many other parts of the world. It was unique in that it was a woman's movement, and women's movements were rare at that time. Its objective was the betterment of the home and community life, things that had hitherto been expected to take care of themselves. It was a rural movement and rural people are generally cautious about taking up a new cause.

It came about in this way: In a day when our infant mortality was appallingly high, Mrs. Adelaide Hoodless of Hamilton lost her baby, and when the doctor said the cause of his death was probably contaminated milk, she felt her son had died because she had not known to take care of him. Mrs. Hoodless was a woman of ability and social influence. She wanted to save other women from a grief like her own; so she determined to do what she could to promote the education of women for homemaking and the care fo their families. She headed a campaign for the teaching of "domestic science" in public schools; and when she was asked to speak at a farmers' conference at the agricultural college, she told her audience that their cattle were fed more scientifically than their families.

A public spirited young farmer of Wentworth County, Erland Lee, was so impressed that he invited Mrs. Hoodless to speak at a ladies' night at his Farmers' Institute at Stoney Creek. The outcome of this was another meeting to make plans for a women's organization to work for better homes just as the men worked for better farming. So the first Women's Institute in the world was organized at Stoney Creek on the night of February 12th, 1897.

For the Institute women themselves, the primary interest at the beginning was a study program about food, home management, and child guidance. They held regular meetings in one another's homes or occasionally in a village hall, and gave talks, read papers or held discussions, sharing what they knew and searching whatever books and periodicals they could find for more expert authority. They brought in speakers and demonstrators from the School of Fine Arts in Hamilton, and later from Macdonald Institute, Guelph. It was the beginning of a new interest in nutrition, a trend to the use of more vegetables and milk and whole cereals in the farm diet. The women were interested in home labor savers. One Institute bought a hand-powered vacuum cleaner - very modern at the time, set it on an express wagon and rented it out to housewives for twenty-five cents a day. Some of their most progressive work was in the field of child study. Papers prepared by mothers three-quarters of a century ago and still on record are amazingly in harmony with the best in child psychology today. Papers dealing with housework are terribly outdated.

In the late 1800s the study of home economics was beginning to catch the imagination of urban women too, partly because Mrs. Hoodless was prodding the universities to take it up. She had persuaded Sir William Macdonald to give funds to establish Macdonald Institute on the campus of the Ontario Agricultural College, and when this school of household science was opened in 1903, primarily for the education of farmers' daughters, for once the rural woman was in the vanguard of a popular women's movement.

In these early days we heard a good deal about what the Women's Institute meant to "the isolated farm woman".A poem, "The Farm Wife", popular at the time, said,
        "She never climbed a mountain,
            She never heard the sea,
        But always watched a winding road
            That wandered aimlessly".
The farm wife who belonged to the Institute no longer stayed at home watching the road. A good deal of her time she was on it, driving with a horse and buggy to a meeting at a neighbor's farm home or in the village or the next township.

Off to the Institute meeting

The road was presenting a new hazard, too - the risk of meeting a "horseless carriage" and having to get out of "the rig" and hold the horse by the bridle till the thing got past. Indeed many Women's Institutes sent resolutions to the government demanding that automobiles be not allowed on country roads.

The Institute not only extended a woman's community over a large area. Because it was non-sectarian in religion it brought together women who never met through their churches; and being non-partisan there were no political arguments to cause trouble. This broadening of the community, and the involvement of more of the people had benefits for the whole family, as the Institute made quite a feature of socials and entertainments and an occasional educational event open to everyone, men and young people as well as women.

Another concern of most Institutes was to carry on the rural tradition of good neighboring. As individuals the members would continue to help a neighbor in need; but they soon found that as a group they could do what no one of them could do alone. For instance, if a woman was ill and unable to do her housework, a neighbor might bring her a basket from her Saturday baking, or drop in for a few hours to do a washing. But this was only makeshift help. Through the Institute a cleaning woman could be provided, or a hired girl to tide over the emergency if there were children to care for.

The women were quick to see that besides doing their best for their children at home, they should take an interest in their welfare at school. This was the day of the one-room rural school with a board of local trustees sometimes chosen because they could be counted on to keep expenses down to a minimum. At first the Institute tried to help the schools by supplying such extras as sanitary drinking cups, playground equipment, sometimes even a piano. Later they learned the better way of persuading the school board to provide these things from the taxes of all the people. They campaigned for health inspection in rural schools and when this was granted some branches sponsored clinics to have children's defects corrected. All of this came long before we had any promise of health insurance, but there is no doubt the Institute's continuous health education had a lot to do with preparing rural people for universal health insurance when the government introduced it later.

In the late 1800s public libraries in rural Ontario were few and far between, and most of them were sadly in need of new books. The Women's Institutes brought in travelling libraries from the Department of Education and used them, sometimes to supplement the stock in the existing local library, sometimes to start a new distributing centre. A popular library might be found operating in a private home, a school, a country store or a cheese factory. An Institute on St. Joseph's Island converted an old jail into what is now a very up-to-date library. The Institute usually provided a woman to act like as librarian. When county libraries were set up, many of the little libraries started by the Institutes continued to serve as book distributing centres for the Community.

At this time when our rural population far exceeded the urban, the majority of Women's Institutes members were farmers' wives; and practically every farmer's wife had her own little butter and egg business, not to use as a source of personal income, but to provide the family groceries, clothing for the children and herself, and such extras as a new parlor carpet. In many families the mother's "butter and egg money" made it possible for the children to go to high school or even to get a start in university. It was natural, then, that the Institute should try to help its members by bringing in a poultry specialist - very often the county representative of the Department of Agriculture - to show women how to cull a flock of hens to find the "good layers"; or an instructor from the Dairy Department at the agricultural college to demonstrate butter making.

The Institutes were interested, too, in making their homes attractive, and they studied home furnishing and decorating as best they could from magazine articles and findings of their own. This was the day of "color schemes" and mission furniture and the new inlaid linoleum and these found their way into the homes of those who could afford them. The women worked on their "home surroundings" too. They exchanged flower seeds and roots and started perennial borders. In a letter drafted to answer the flood of inquiries coming to the government about the new women's organization, Dr. George Creelman of the Ontario Agricultural College wrote:

"In Ontario we have been so busy cleaning up land and growing out of the log cabin period that we have had little time to attend to the development of the beautiful about our homes. Now we are free from the long grind. Wood piles are relegated to the rear. Vines now clamber over the porches, lawns are cut and trees are planted along the lanes. Flowers are grown in front instead of vegetables, and such homes become an expression of the culture of the inhabitants and preach a sermon to the passer-by."

Programs were not limited to practical or technical interests. Along with Home Economics and Agriculture there were standing commitees on Education. Legislation and Immigration. Many Institutes made a feature of book reviews. And all the time the members were gaining experience in public speaking. Looking back now, as I remember them, it seems that a high proportion of the early Institute devotees were natural orators. One incident where their ability served the community well got a lot of publicity. In a Northern Ontario district there was keen dissatisfaction about a government proposed roadway. Feeling was running high and officials from the Department of Highways were asked to come to a public meeting where the issue could be debated. The officials came and the men who were expected to present the case of the people, but who had never done such a thing before, "lost their nerve" and were practically tongue-tied. Not so the women! In their Institute meetings they had learned to talk to an audience; they understood their road problem as well as anyone; and the community was happy to have them for spokesmen. After a lively debate the differences were settled.

Whatever new interests were added to Institute programs, the study of homemaking continued, the subjects changing to keep pace with changing conditions. In 1912 demonstration-lecture courses in Foods, Sewing and Home Nursing were introduced, with itinerant instructors going the rounds of five neighboring communities teaching one day in each place to give a course of ten lessons. In the winter, in co-operation with the county representative of the Department of Agriculture, courses in home economics for girls were held simultaneously with courses in agriculture for young men. Sometimes it was difficult to find places for classrooms - one of the most unusual being a hall over a blacksmith shop where lecturers had to compete with the beat of the blacksmith's hammer downstairs. But the courses were good. Along with home economics and agriculture, the young people - young men and girls together, studied English and civics and debating and music. It is not surprising that some of the men and women in later years promoting Community Colleges, felt their first thirst for education in these short courses years ago.

When World War 1 began in 1914, the Women's Institutes immediately turned to "war work". They served and knitted for the Red Cross. They set up canning centres and made jam to send to Britain. They financed a field kitchen, a hospital ship and a motor ambulance. It is reported that their total contribution was valued at $4,000,000. When military priorities left few farm laborers in the country, farm women and girls went into the fields to help produce more wheat and beef and bacon. The same sort of service was repeated in the second World War. Since then the Women's Institute has developed a strong feeling of world-wide sympathy and responsability, and along with other country women, in affiliation with the Associated Country Women of the World, our Institutes work for peace and human welfare and progress in countries less privileged than ours.

But the Ontario Women's Institutes still major in education for family living; and one of the best things they do is to support and provide local leaders for Girls' 4H Homemaking Clubs under the supervision of their county home economists. Last year Ontario had 16,569 girls taking this most effective and popular training. We are proud of this, but we don't forget that, as with many of our causes for thanksgiving, we are pensioners of the past. We know something of our debt to the wise and steadfast women who guided our organization through its earlier years.

MOTOR CARS

by Norman McPherson

In the early years the motorcar was referred to by several names: motor vehicle, horseless carriage, autocar, and sometimes by less complimentary terms. It was well into this century before general usage settled on the terms used today: automobile, motorcar and finally just car. Most of the early experimenting with motorized vehicles was done on the continent of Europe. The internal combustion engine was invented in Germany by Gottlieb Daimler; and Levassor in France devised the transmission system. Though there has been vast improvement in the transmission over the years, it remains in principle what Levassor developed — a clutch, a gear-box, and a differential. During the nineties of last century the improvement of motorcar construction was greatly encouraged by well publicized races. In 1895 a race was organized by the Petit Journal from Paris to Bordeaux and back, a distance of 744 miles. Believe it or not, the leading car covered the distance with the breath-taking speed of 15 miles an hour! As time went on other races international in scope were held between Paris and Vienna. Engines were gradually improved until by 1908 four cylinder engines were developing 60 horse power or even more.

It was Henry Ford, however, who made the motorcar really popular. By introducing the assembly line method of construction, he brought the price of a car down to what an ordinary citizen could afford. My memory goes back to the time when a new Ford could be bought for $425; but I believe that at one time they were selling for less than that. The old Ford car was a sturdy and uncomplicated vehicle. When you pressed down on the clutch the car was in low gear; when you released the pedal it was in high gear. Its best speed was twenty miles an hour. At the Chicago World's Fair early in the century the Ford car was advertised by a record which repeated over and over again, "I take you there, I bring you back".

To be sure, if you came to a steep hill, you might have to turn around and back up. But what did that matter? It got you to the top, and that was the main thing.

Cranking a car, especially in winter, was quite a problem. For one thing, you had to be careful that the crank didn't kick back and break your arm. To prevent it from kicking back, there was a gadget on some cars to retard the spark for starting, and advance it for steady driving.

I remember one make of car (I think it was a Russell-Knight) that had a special device to make starting easy. When you opened the hood (it opened from the side) you saw a row of pet--cocks, one on each cylinder. To start the motor you opened the first pet-cock, poured in a little gasoline from a bottle you kept for the purpose, and closed the pet-cock. Then you opened the second pet-cock, poured in gasoline, and closed it. And so on until all the cylinders had been primed. You then closed the hood and cranked the engine. This priming of each cylinder was the early forerunner of the automatic choke. Sometimes it didn't work either, and you had to go through the routine of priming and cranking all over again.

Night driving in the early days was none too easy. The coal--oil lamps which were installed in the earliest cars revealed very little of the road ahead. Without old Dobbin's good eyes to keep you on the road, you were likely to find yourself in the ditch. Following the oil lamps, came the acetylene headlights, which, though dangerous, were a decided improvement. On one of the running-boards was a tank in which the gas was generated. The tank was partly filled with carbide, and when you wanted to use the lights you turned on a small tap, which permitted water to drip on the carbide. The result was an inflammable gas which you then lit in each of the headlights. To extinguish the lights you simply turned off the water and gradually the lights would die down.

The final improvement before batteries were installed in cars, was the electric headlights with current derived from the magneto. This worked fine, except when you were going up a hill. As you struggled to the top of the hill the car would go more and more slowly (in a modern car you would scarcely notice the grade) and the lights would become dimmer and dimmer, until at the top, where there was sure to be a wandering cow or a peripatetic pig, you were almost blind.

Before detachable rims were invented, tires were even more of a problem. I remember one trip in an old Ford – an old tin Lizzie – from St. Thomas to London. It was only nineteen miles, but it took us all night. We had six flat tires on the way. When a tire went flat, we had to jack up the car, pry the tire off the rim, remove the inner tube, find the puncture (not an easy thing in the dark) apply glue and a patch, wait for the glue to harden, put the tire back on the rim, and pump it up.

None of the roads was paved. A woman had to wear a scarf over her head to keep the dust out of her hair; and both men and women wore light coats called dusters. But the dust got in your eyes, your nose, your ears, and down your neck. The polluted air of today is refreshing compared with the dust-laden air of yesterday. And when it wasn't dust you had to contend with, it was mud. After a heavy rain many of the roads were almost impassable. The mud holes were so deep that sometimes the rear wheels of a car would sink almost up to the axle. Farmers made a good thing out of dragging cars out of the mud with a team of horses.

Motoring in the old days was an adventure. Early motorcars were capricious and unreliable contraptions. When you set out on the road you never knew what might happen. If it wasn't the tires, it was mechanical trouble. To operate them properly, a man had to be something of a mechanic. But they became more efficient over the years.

Nothing has improved more than motorcars. In ease of operation, reliability, comfort, appearance – if motorcars were not so common today we would consider them marvels of engineering. The modern motorcar is vastly superior to the old tin Lizzie except in one regard, safety. As governments permitted higher and higher speeds on our highways, manufacturers produced flimsier and flimsier cars.

Here is a true story.

Years ago I was driving on highway 2 when I had to stop on a Y for two cars going south. As I waited I became aware of a rapidly increasing roar behind me. I glanced in the rear-view mirror to see an old Ford sedan weaving crazily from side to side of the roadway and approaching at high speed. I was sure that it was going to crash into the back of my car. But at the last moment it swerved violently to the left, so violently that the front wheels cramped and it turned two complete somersaults and rolled over three times, ending in the ditch. Five men, all very drunk, and one dog, completely sober, scrambled out. Not one of them had suffered any serious injury.

What would happen to them in a modern car that performed such unaccustomed capers? Undoubtedly they would all be crushed and bloody corpses embedded in a shapeless mass of twisted steel.

But let us get back to the period under consideration. Maurice H. Park (Mike for short) recounted to me the following story of an epic journey in one of the old cars in the early years of the century. The distance covered was only about sixty miles, but it took five days. I tell the story in Mike's words.

Uncle Jim's Folly

If you have ever watched me trying to change a tire today, you would never believe that at one time I was quite a mechanic. And somehow or other — I have forgotten how — I had learned to operate an automobile before I was out of high school. One day my uncle, who lived in Sutton, a small town on the south shore of Lake Simcoe, called on me for help.

"Mike," he said, "I have a job for you."

"Very good, sir."

"You know how to drive an auty-mobile? "

"I sure do."

"I saw an advertisement for a secondhand auty-mobile in the Peterborough newspaper, and I bought the consarned thing by mail. I want you to bring it home for me."

How trusting people were in those days, buying a used car sight unseen!

"Glad to, sir," I said.

"It's not more than sixty miles by road. If you take the train to Peterborough in the morning, you should be back here before supper."

As far as I can remember, the car was an early Russell touring car, much higher off the ground than a modern car, with coal-oil lamps on each side of the hood, and detachable side curtains which could be put on when it rained.

For company I took along my younger brother, Ernie. He was as taciturn as I was voluble. When he was annoyed, he would go through the motion of spitting, but without emitting any saliva. A sort of dry run, if you know what I mean. But he could express more by one explosive expectoration than I could by a stream of cuss words. We arrived in Peterborough late in the morning, had dinner at the hotel, and started for home in the newly purchased automobile about 2:30 in the afternoon. We made quite a commotion driving up the main street, with youngsters yelling at us, horses shying, and dogs barking. But at last we got out on the country road and increased our speed to twenty miles an hour.

At this exhilarating rate of progress we kicked up a rooster's tail of dust and scared the devil out of chickens that were peacefully pecking along the roadside. It was a glorious feeling, no horse jogging along ahead lazily whisking its tail, just the open road beckoning us over the next hill. It would be no time at all until we would be making a triumphal entry into Sutton, like Caesar returning to Rome after a successful campaign in Gaul.

But in a swamp near Omemee, before we had gone twenty miles, we hit a bump in the road, and something went wrong. The engine stopped dead. When we cranked it and let in the clutch, it stopped again. For hours we worked, tightening this and disassembling that. Lying on our backs on the stony road, we examined the transmission from the engine to the rear axle. And at last when it was almost dark we discovered the trouble in the gear box. The shaft of one of the gears was badly bent. Ernie looked at it and spat twice vigorously, while I turned the air blue with curses. Nothing could be done about it that night, so we curled up, one on each seat of the car, and went to sleep.

In the morning we walked back a hundred yards or so and spotted a farmhouse a quarter of a mile away. How a farmer could help us we did not know. But we got the mangled gear and took it with us to the farmhouse.

When we told our troubles to the farmer, he laughed.

"You look like decent lads," he said. "What are you doing with an invention of the devil like that? Scaring the daylights out of horses, and disturbing peaceful cattle in the fields. Why don't you get yourselves a nice horse and buggy? "

"It isn't ours, sir," said I.

67

"Whose is it? "

"Our uncle's, sir. We're just driving it home for him. He just bought it."

"I see."

"It broke down."

"The darned things always do."

"We're wondering if you could help us."

"What's wrong with it? "

We showed him the twisted shaft. By a miracle, that sort of miracle that often rescues drunks and arrant fools from trouble, the farmer happened to have a forge in the barn. After the farmer's wife had given us breakfast, the first food we had eaten since we left Peterborough, we went to the barn and the farmer got the forge going. In due time he succeeded in hammering the gear shaft into shape. But back at the car it took us more than an hour to assemble the gears and make everything ready for another start.

When we were approaching Lindsay we found ourselves confronted by a steep hill. It was apparent that we would have to negotiate the hill on low gear. I threw out the clutch and jammed the gear-shift lever into the low-gear position. But when I let the clutch in again there was a bang and a clatter, and the car slid to a standstill.

This time we found that it was the clutch that had gone wrong. One of the discs was so badly cracked that it would have to be replaced.

I stayed with the car while my brother, spitting with anger and frustration all the way, walked a mile or so into Lindsay and found a garage — or rather, an establishment that was part garage and part blacksmith shop. The garage mechanic towed us in, and we were in Lindsay two days while a new part was ordered from the factory.

Once more on the road, we were bowling along at a good clip when bang! one of the front tires blew out. It not only blew out, but it came right off the rim, rolled across the road like a hoop, and collapsed in the ditch. But that was not all. Thrown out of control, the car followed the tire, and crashed into the fence, which was one of those old snake fences made of rails. One of the rails jammed into the radiator.

Ernie didn't spit. He said, "Dod-dash-it! "

We retrieved the tire, patched it, put it back on the rim, and pumped it up. But when I backed the car onto the road, we found that the radiator was leaking badly. Once more unbelievable luck favored us. In the back of the car there just happened to be a pail, and not fifty yards ahead by the side of the road was a pool of water. We filled the radiator with water, and once more were on our way. But whenever we saw a stream or a pool of water we stopped and filled the radiator. It was leaking almost as fast as we could fill it.

In this uncertain manner we progressed as far as Beaverton, where we found, not a garage mechanic, but a plumber who was brave enough to undertake the almost impossible task of straightening out the radiator and soldering it. He worked the remainder of the day and well into the afternoon of the following day before he got it reasonably watertight.

"Well, there she is, boys," he said, rubbing the sweat from his forehead with an oily rag. "She'll be a bit thirsty. But watch her and you'll be all right."

With this rather dubious assurance, we cranked the motor, and backed out of the plumber's lane. We were in high spirits when we found ourselves once again on the open road. Ernie yelled "Whoopie! " and I burst into song. We had only a few more miles to go, and we were sure that our troubles were over.

But not so.

When we were within three or four miles of our destination we were startled by ominous screeches and groans from the bowels of the cantankerous machine which we were operating, and again we coasted to a halt.

We climbed down from the stationary automobile and looked at it. Ernie spat more explosively than I ever before heard him. And I scratched my head. What was wrong with the darned thing this time?

A farmer who had been working in a nearby field vaulted the fence and came up to us. He was a big, good-natured fellow with a slow drawling voice.

"Well, boys, what's your trouble? " he asked.

"We don't know, sir," I said.

"Are you out of gasoline? "

"No. I had her filled up before we left Beaverton."

"Is she sparking all right? "

"I don't think that's the trouble. There was too much noise when she stopped. I think something is busted."

"Well, let's have a look."

The farmer went to the front of the car, lifted up the hood, and said "My God! "

"What's the matter? " both Ernie and I asked anxiously.

"Where's the engine? "

"The engine? "

"Yes. Where is it? "

We went forward and looked. Where the motor should have been there was nothing but empty space.

"Well," the farmer repeated in his slow voice,

"What's happened to the engine? "

"I guess we lost it," I said.

"You can't lose something as big as an engine. It must be around somewhere."

We found the engine forty or fifty yards back on the road.

"Well," said the farmer grinning, "that's that. You can't make much headway without a motor. How far are you going? "

"To Sutton."

"I can't take you there today. But you come up to the house. The wife will put you up for the night. And in the morning I'll hitch up a team and tow you into Sutton."

That is how we arrived at our destination, after five days and five nights on the road. The car never made another trip. It was deposited in the middle of my uncle's front lawn. His wife made him remove the top, and she filled the seats with potted geraniums. And somebody (nobody ever knew who) put a sign in front of the old jalopy which read: "Uncle Jim's Folly."

Retired

REMEMBER WHO YOU ARE

by Kay Henderson

Believe me, I always did, for I was never allowed to forget it. Being reared in a Methodist country parsonage at the turn of the century was not conducive to forgetting that you were the minister's daughter. It was a way of life long gone now.

There was papa, the Rev. William Winters Ryan, handsome and forceful, known as the Silver Tongued Orator of the North, a hell-fire preacher of his day. He had blue eyes and beautiful white hair, (nicer even than Lloyd George's), which always had blueing added to the rinse water to make it look even whiter. He was always doing something with his facial hair too. Sometimes it would be Dundreary side whiskers, or a beautiful flowing moustache, or even a full beard. I adored my papa but I really could have done without being kissed with all that hair. Papa as a young lad had come on a sailing ship from Kilkenny to New York City and then walked along the Erie Canal, "with me bundle on me shoulder", all the way to what is the Goderich district today, to join his half-brothers. Papa literally was the boy who carried a book on his plough, and was the first young man in the district to own an oil lamp for he studied at night. He went to Victoria College when it was still in Cobourg and then became a circuit rider or saddle-bag preacher.

There was mamma, so tall and slender with lustrous dark eyes and dark hair in an immaculate French roll. She had a perfect figure for the 1900s but she did wear bosom cheaters, for as I grew older I often ironed those little rows of starched embroidery frills, I remember the wide leather belts with big buckles to show off her slender waist, and the long skirts, which swept the sidewalk and had a ruching of horse-hair inside at the hem. There was a special little brush to clean off the mud and dust picked up on the street. I thought my mamma very elegant. She loved hats, which of course everyone wore. No lady would appear on the street without a hat and gloves. And being poor, as we were, mamma was always refurbishing some hat. Well do we remember the tuneful humming which went on during the process and a certain triumphant revving up when all was going well.

My wonderful mother, I am sure, never realized when she married her adored William, all that being a minister's wife would entail. Once she told me that the first time she had to lead a women's meeting she was so glad it was the custom to kneel at one's chair for prayer, for if she had had to stand up she didn't think she could have done it.

And there was I, born in the first month of the new century — the first child in the second family. The others kept coming along at intervals until I was twelve. I first saw the light of day in Victoria Harbour on Georgian Bay, and they tell that the first time papa clapped eyes on me he exclaimed, "Glory be to God, I've got an Irishman at last." I must have been an excessively homely infant with a map like Paddy's pig. I have no memories of Victoria Harbour, only the stories I heard of my baby days. I loved to hear the tales of papa's encounters with the liquor enterprises, which hated his fiery temperance sermons. Many's the time they surrounded the house in the dark, beating tin pans and shouting threats and rude imprecations. I understand that Victoria Harbour is a very different place today.

* * *

My own memories begin when I was nearing three and we moved to Burk's Falls. I see myself, a small solitary figure swinging on the front gate and a strange lady stopping to say, "You must be the new minister's little girl." They tell that I replied, "I'm Kathleen, and he's not new. He's my papa, and we've always had him." It was there I first became aware of parishioners. I remember the black satin laps I had to sit on, the bosoms with jet brooches and the bonnets with twinkling jet beads. I was very intrigued with all the dainty muffs which smelt heavenly and invariably had a lace handkerchief peeping from the end. A baby brother was born there and later a second brother. They figured largely in my life for I learned early that being a minister's daughter sets one apart, a rather lonely position, so that the family circle becomes everything. I was never

Kay in those days, always Kathleen. Shortening of names was not allowed. Remember who you are! I have wondered if that is why I had so many nick-names. "Child of the Century" was a favourite because of the month of my birth, "Little Morning Face", or "Old Grogram Eyes".

It is hard to choose among all the memories that throng my mind when I was becoming aware of so much for the first time. The church was next to the house and I see two of my half-sisters dusting the pews for Sunday. Doubtless they had taken the two of us with them to get us out of Mamma's hair. I ran up and down the aisles enjoying the splashes of colour on me from the church windows, while my small brother in his bright red dress was set on a chair behind the pulpit to play at being papa. He shouted and pounded the pulpit in most satisfying fashion. When my sisters were finished, Jennie said, "Come now, time for Nennie's little bishop to go home."

I see the kitchen in the lamplight. Papa is not there. He is doubtless out at one of his country appointments. Mamma is bathing the baby and I am sitting on the dog. This was Babe, the fat black water spaniel, a tolerant companion and seat for a small three year old. Suddenly there is a knock at the door. When mamma opens it there stands a tramp, the dreaded bogeyman of my youth. Do they still have tramps in the country to-day? This one wanted something to eat and he knew the parsonage was the right place to ask. While the man ate, Babe waddled over stumpy tail wagging, to sniff a pant leg, and I still see mamma once the door was shut, leaning there, her hand at her breast, and saying scornfully, "Some watch dog."

I remember too a moment of disgrace. It happened when mamma was hostess to the Ladies' Aid and the meeting was in the front parlour. Andrew and I were dressed in our best and I was to see he didn't get into mischief till time for refreshments, when we would be on display. Remember who you are ! We still have a picture of us as we were then, with him in his white embroidered dress and little white kid boots. Somehow he managed to get out on the back porch and dance happily up and down in a pan of ashes. Obviously mamma was called for but how to get up the courage to interrupt the meeting!! I stood in the hall smelling the dust from the chenille portieres, finally pushed them aside and led the culprit up to mamma.

Remember who you are

Even in my embarrassment I remembered to use one of my new 'big people' words. "Now, see the predicament he's got himself into." As they would say today, the meeting 'broke up'.

At least a couple of summers were spent on an island in Ahmic Lake. It was a place of pure joy, the cottage at the top of the steep island all covered with evergreens. In good weather we ate our meals on the verandah, looking out across the water to the wild country around. Each morning someone got into the skiff to go across to the mainland farm for milk, butter and eggs. Often I was allowed to go along and I remember especially the big bullfrog who always greeted us, "Garrumph, garrumph". We had to walk through the cow pasture and there were many mushrooms which the farmers would not eat, so mamma always took along a basket to gather them. Even today a well broiled mushroom takes me back.

Going out in the skiff was a special treat for me. Sometimes papa would take me after supper as the fish began to rise and twilight crept over the still water. It was the purest bliss to sit in the stern, listening to the quiet plop of the oars, a line grasped in my small hand, waiting for that momentous tug which meant a fish. Of course, I could not have lost it for the line was tied to the thwart. It is all mixed up with the smell of the water and the pines. Even the cushions were stuffed with pine needles, and I particularly treasured one which bore the legend, "For you I pine, and then I balsam".

* * *

Then we moved to Rocklyn and I was six. I lived happily all summer with the knowledge that when September came I would go to school with the other children, only to discover when the time came that it was the considered opinion of the 'big people' that it was too far for my short legs to carry me. So inconsolable was I that it was decided mamma should begin my letters and numbers at home. Papa bought me a scribbler and pencil, a slate with a box of slate pencils and a small sponge, and I was in business. Learning to count was painful, but learning to read was fulfillment and I could hardly wait to be shown. When I could manage to read something I didn't already know by heart it was my biggest step forward from being a baby. My other accomplishment when I was six was beginning to iron. The board was laid on the seats of two chairs and there was a very small flat-iron, just my size. I began on the baby's nappies, progressed to papa's handkerchiefs and then to linen serviettes, which were much harder and dampened my enthusiasm. How patient mamma was, isolated in the country without even the store or the church close by. Luckily, it was only for one year, as papa was not well and had a sabbatical in Toronto.

That next year in Toronto represented something very special, for my baby sister was born. Life would never be exactly the same again. I was seven but I still did not go to regular school. It was considered too far, or too dangerous crossing streets, so I was sent to a private kindergarten which I could reach by just walking round the block. Mercy, was that dull! At home it was much better for my two small brothers and I played all sorts of exciting games; we made up our own for we were never lacking in imagination. We still had a horse and buggy and we lived in East Toronto on Swanwick Avenue on the very eastern edge of the city. Sometimes papa would be visiting minister at an out-lying church. Then I would be dressed in my starchy best and away we would go through the sunny summer weather, papa and I. How is it that the sun always seems to have been shining then? I sit here pondering on the Toronto of sixty-five years ago, and what it is like now, and think surely I must soon begin to feel old.

* * *

When we moved to Mattawa a whole new life began. We lived at the confluence of the Mattawa River and the mighty Ottawa, which rolled in majesty past the bottom of our garden and was forbidden territory. I was eight: I went to regular school; and I learned with great interest about Catholics and French--Canadians. I wasn't allowed to play with little Dolly Valois across the street because she was French-Canadian and a Catholic. Remember who you are! School was very exciting and I forged ahead, for of course, I could already read and write. We had a big yard full of pine trees and a most wonderful swing which could go so high one almost touched the branches and looked out over the river. We always seemed to have a swing no matter where we lived, a swing and dogs. Here again, I used to go with papa to his country appointments and I particularly remember the hardness of kneeling on the bare wood at the altar rail, and the peculiar taste of the communion wine. I knelt with bowed head wondering if a curse from heaven would fall on me if I did not drain the small glass.

I think Mattawa was the place where the 'dressing up box' began. Into it went all the most unsuitable things from the missionary barrels which used to arrive every now and then from Toronto. I always dreaded their arrival in case they might contain something considered suitable for me to wear, but the things for the 'dressing up box' were great — old evening gowns and feather boas and tail coats and top hats. Mamma never could figure out how the Toronto people could think these suitable for country parsonages. I think too that Mattawa was the place where we became 'us' against 'them', and thus it remained till we all grew up, for there was no doubt in our minds that the grown-ups represented the enemy, no matter how much we loved our own 'big people'. We were all loved and cherished, no doubt of that, but papa came first, no doubt of that either. Papa was always correcting one's pronunciation, laying particular emphasis on the letters 'i' and 'e'. He always seemed to be in his garden if he wasn't in his study. I would come running through the gate and he would look up and say, "And where have you been, stravagin' up the street? Into the house with you this minute. Your hair looks like a hurrah's nest. Anyone would think your grandmother had bare feet." Remember who you are!

Next, we moved to Powassan and I was ten and eleven. School became ever more absorbing to me, though I was always being reproved for being so fidgety. It was hard to keep still when life was so exciting. Sunday was the worst for it was church all day. For breakfast we got the texts and admonitions. At church there was the long, fiery sermon which seemed endless. But one must attend closely for one would rather sink through the floor than have papa suddenly pause, looking over his glasses, and say, "Ka-a-athleen, be still." With dinner we got the sermon over again with any additional things papa had not had time for in church and were catechized as to texts, hymns and lessons we had learned therefrom. I particularly remember that when I had on my crisp white dress and blue satin sash, I went just before church into the garden where the Sweet Mary or Costmary plant grew, and picked leaves to be laid in bible and hymn book to mark the proper places. "So that," I thought, "is why it's called Bible Leaf." After Sunday dinner which was always left in the oven, came Sunday School and by the time supper was reached we were full to the brim with Sunday. Still, of course, there was sometimes evening service and always the customary family prayers at bedtime.

But life was good and the blood ran singing through the veins. I can feel my small stout boots or moccasins pelting along the wooden sidewalk on the way home from school, racing to see who would be first home to mamma and home-made bread and milk or cocoa. One would be sent to tap politely on the study door. There papa sat, sipping tea from his big moustache cup, and interrogating each of us as to how our day had gone. Mouths full of goodness, we answered all questions regardless.

Those were horse and buggy or cutter days and I still can hardly figure how we all crowded into that buggy. Mamma sat by papa; Margaret sat on mamma; I sat between their feet and the two boys sat in the luggage compartment with their feet dangling over the stony road, but where were the berry buckets packed full of lunch? Under the seat? To go to the bush for berry picking was pure bliss; it meant standing in a burnt-over clearing in the hot sun with the delicious smell of the ripe raspberries all round and a little bird singing in a tree top, "Oh, Canada, Canada, Canada," or sitting on sun-warmed rocks eating those home-made sandwiches with the odour of fresh blueberries and crushed lichen all about as one looked out across some northern lake. We would go rattling along the gravel road, singing, "Shall we gather at the river," or "From Greenland's icy mountains," when papa would suddenly wave his whip dramatically and say, "Nice looking crop of turnips there, wife." I watched for the look of pained distaste on mamma's face, for we all knew that the cellar would be well stocked with whatever root vegetables were in surplus supply. The farmers had a regrettable habit of paying their dues in kind rather than cash, and we might be eating turnips all winter. In the winter it was the cutter with the black bear rug over the seat and the voluminous buffalo robe to cover us. We sped along the country roads with the sleigh bells jingling merrily and clods of snow from the horse's hooves pelting against the cutter. If the wind got too cold one hid under the robe with the hot bricks and it smelt of horse, and animal skins and dust, and gave a very secure feeling.

Paying her dues

In the spring someone would always be having a sugaring-off. Have you ever ridden on the horse-drawn pung sleigh, helping to gather the sap into the big barrel, or had maple taffy made by pouring blobs of thick syrup into the snow? We twisted it onto a small stick and licked blissfully. In the summer were the strawberry festivals and this meant home-made ice cream. Of course, we made ice cream for birthdays and other special occasions too and what a do with all that salt and ice and the endless turning of the handle! But that was real ice cream with plenty of eggs and fresh strawberries or maybe maple syrup in it, not the air-filled concoction one gets today. We had ice cream also at the Sunday School picnic which was a summer day of simple sports and games, ending with a fabulous spread of all the best cooking in the congregation. On the way home the buggy was full of sleeping children. Outside of the 12th of July with its fifes and drums, the only other exciting event was when the circus came to town with its garish parade down Main Street. "Calathumpian" parade, there was a new word for my vocabulary, but it's not in the dictionary. We were allowed to view the parade but not to go to the performance. Papa did not approve of such worldly affairs. Remember who you are!

* * *

King Edward died too and caused much furious activity. Mamma was too late to get any purple sateen but not to be outdone, she bought many yards of cheesecloth and dyed it herself. I still can feel about me the quiet emptiness of the church with its own special atmosphere, as I helped mamma drape this in festoons round the altar rail for the memorial service. That cheesecloth was great in the 'dressing-up box' afterwards though; it made fine trains and especially fine turbans. Most exciting of all was that Halley's Comet came and papa bought a spyglass. I think I was ten. We were allowed to creep through the bedroom window on to the verandah roof in our night clothes to watch this great thing with the fiery tail in the sky. I still recall the rough feeling of the shingles on my little bare bottom. Papa said, "Remember children, this happens only once in seventy-five years, so you may possibly see it again, but your mother and I never will." Shall I see it in 1985?

Winters were great too with all that northern snow to romp in and make snowmen and go tobogganing. How depressing it must have been for mamma to have the kitchen draped with four sets of steaming wet clothes. Winter also meant Christmas with the Sunday School concert complete with Santa Claus, the big glittering tree and small parcels and net sacks of sweets for each child, and the Christmas concert with many small, earnest performers. At home Christmas meant going with papa and the toboggan and axe to the bush for the tree. It touched the ceiling and was hung with all the glitter we could afford and also the popcorn and cranberry chains which we made ourselves. Some of those old tree ornaments still survive today. We were not allowed to get up on Christmas morning till papa was heard running through the house with the ringing sleigh bells, crying "Santa Claus is here." Then we pattered down to the mantel for our long black stockings, full to the top, with the exceptional treat of an orange in the toe. All four got into one bed with our cold toes toward the middle, and investigated our treasures — such innocent happiness and so seldom encountered today. We had to be properly dressed and have a proper breakfast and family prayers before it was time for the tree and all those mysterious parcels. Then all must be tidied away before the fabulous Christmas dinner with every possible adjunct, except of course, wine. No alcohol in the parsonage! Remember who you are! I always saved my book till after dinner and the washing up. Every Christmas and birthday I got a book, brand new, and I never untied it till last, speculating in ecstasy all day as to what it might be. Thus another of my childhood nicknames, "Little Bookworm".

Of course, living in a parsonage meant lots of company at table. This brought about a code which we used at the dinner table, (FHB) family hold back, or (MIK) more in the kitchen. We still use it in fun, and I was reminded just the other day of my smallest brother running into the kitchen crying out, "Mamma, Mamma, papa's brother is here." Of course, the visiting clergyman at the door had simply said, "Is Brother Ryan home?" There were often quiet weddings in the parlour too and someone brought in to act as witness. The fee from all weddings traditionally belonged to the minister's wife, so mamma had her own little secret hoard.

Now something cataclysmic happened. Papa retired from the ministry after all those years of selfless service, and became Superintendent for the Children's Aid Society for northern Ontario. Now we had a house of our very own which nevertheless was always a sort of way-station for homeless Children's Aid waifs, and mamma was busier than ever. Then I was twelve and my last brother was born. In North Bay which seemed to me an enormous community, I went to school in a big brick building and, undoubtedly most momentous of all, I discovered the Public Library. I was led there by a new school chum and gazed at the Andrew Carnegie Memorial Library, unable to believe that it contained nothing but books. I rushed home and burst in on mamma with my news that you could borrow any book and it didn't cost anything. From then on my school work was done, my chores finished in jig time and my week zeroed in on Saturday's visit to the library. Soon I was allowed to take home two books a week and my love affair with the Public Library persists to this day.

We went to a big brick church and it seemed very odd to be sitting in the pew with papa. But we were still a minister's children; it was still "Remember who you are". This would never change till we moved to the city. There was a big indoor rink with a band, and on Friday nights I was allowed to go skating. I adored it for the music in my feet was already beginning to cause trouble. No dancing in a good Methodist household such as ours! Once the skating was over there would be a moccasin dance on the ice and I would keep running into the other part of the building where papa was curling, to see if he was ready to walk me home. What a magnificent figure he cut in his coon coat and sealskin cap!

But the best skating was on Lake Nipissing. Word would go round that the wind had cleared a good patch of ice, and then there would be a big driftwood fire on the beach, silent skating in the starry darkness and hot drinks round the fire. And there were the snowshoeing expeditions on Saturday afternoons or in the holidays. Off into the bush we would trek complete with packets of sandwiches which would soon be frozen solid, but we didn't mind as we sat round a little camp fire in the snow. There would be evening sleigh ride parties from the church into the country where some group of worthy church matrons would be putting on a bean or chicken supper to raise money. The sleighs for this were long with a bench on either side, hay under your feet and rugs to cover you. We went singing through the star-filled night with the jingling bells on the horses for accompaniment.

Soon I would be thirteen and that was a matter for much thought. So much more was expected of a teenager. "You're a big girl now. Why, you're almost thirteen years old." In that year too something literally out of my world happened. My eldest half-sister went to Japan as a teacher and a missionary. Japan! In 1973 that's nothing, right? But in 1913? Suddenly the maps in the atlas became much more interesting and geography took on a whole new aspect. Through this began an interest in things Oriental which persists to this day.

A couple of summers we rented a shacky old house, with out-door kitchen, on the beach about three miles from town, and set up our tents. It was just sand and pine trees and wild raspberries, with a big vegetable garden on the other side of the highway, but it was very heaven. We ran wild, swimming, and picking berries, learning to manage a canoe, trying to ride the horse bareback, and always sitting round a beach fire before bed. To sleep in a tent with the breeze from the lake wafting the scent of pines over you and to wake ravenous for your breakfast, what more could a growing child ask?

Then suddenly it seemed the War came, and I was fourteen, passed my High School Entrance, nearly died of typhoid fever and had all my hair shaved off. Those long weeks of convalescence gave me hours upon hours to ponder the fact that my life was about to change drastically. Just starting High School among the big kids was a thing in itself, but the reluctant realization that the upcoming years meant I would be no longer one of 'us' but one of 'them' was very troubling. "Standing with reluctant feet where the brook and river meet", that was I. So ends the story of growing up at the turn of the century, but a wonderful thing has happened. Since I began to talk of writing this the whole family has got into the act, telling me not to forget this or that, and thus though relentless time has inevitable turned us into 'big people', now I know we are still 'us'. Mamma was right in saying "Remember who you are", and this journey into the past has made me better understand the me of today. I have left out far more than I have dared to put in for it kept wanting to make itself into a book. Now at last at seventy-three I am literally "Old Grogram Eyes", and if my recollections of the early 1900's give anyone else pleasure or amusement, or remind them of their own childhood, I am more than content.

DISEASES, CURES, AND DEATH

by Adrian Macdonald

Though babies were produced in quantity in the nineties, nature had its own method of birth control. Or if not birth control, at least of limiting the population. Many children died of one disease or another before reaching maturity. Diphtheria, typhoid, scarlet fever, whooping cough (sometimes fatal) all took their dreadful toll in the days before antibiotics and immunization shots. Methods of prevention were haphazard, and methods of cure were often ineffective.

The family doctor of the period, however, did his best. And in one regard at least he could teach his modern counterpart a lesson. His devotion to his patients was beyond praise. When you called your doctor on the telephone (telephones became common in the early years of the twentieth century) you got him if he was at all available. You were not told by some uninterested answering service that "Dr. So-and-so is not on call today." And night or day, winter or summer, fair weather or foul, he would hitch up his old nag and come to your assistance if you really needed him.

What the doctor of the period lacked in scientific knowledge, he made up for in human understanding. He was a practical psychologist, with a wealth of knowledge of the quirks and oddities of human nature. He knew his patients thoroughly, and often their parents and their grandparents. Wise and understanding, he often accomplished more in the sick-room by his reassuring presence than the modern doctor can achieve with his multiplicity of expensive pills.

Sir William Osler, who was born at Bond Head, a village a few miles north of Toronto, and who lived to become one of the most famous doctors of all time, imprinted his image on the medical profession of the period. Though he spent most of his life lecturing to students in medical colleges in the United States and Britain, he was the impersonation, the pattern of the perfect general practitioner, the all round family doctor.

He was shrewd, kindly, thoroughly acquainted with every phase of medicine (an impossibility today) and devoted to his profession. His book, "The Principles and Practice of Medicine," first published in 1892, was for many years a textbook in medical schools all over the world.

With universal medical insurance, most doctors today have too many patients. In an effort to conserve their energies, they are forced to resort to unsatisfactory practices. What happens when someone becomes ill? He or some member of his family calls the doctor. The doctor listens, asks three or four questions, and very often makes his diagnosis and suggests treatment over the telephone. The traditional patient-doctor relationship has largely disappeared. It would be more satisfactory if a computer were set up in a convenient location and programmed by a committee of outstanding specialists. When you got sick you would just call the computer centre and retail your symptoms to the person in charge. He would feed your symptoms into the computer, and pop! out would come the diagnosis and treatment in a jiffy.

> There was an old man with the flu,
> Who said, now what shall I du?
> His wife said just call,
> No trouble at all,
> And let the computer compu!

In the nineties smallpox had, of course, been checked by vaccination; and cholera, the curse of pioneer days, by sanitation and perpetual vigilance. But most children, even if they escaped the more serious diseases, went through measles, mumps, chicken-pox, and colic. The symptoms of colic were a pain in the stomach usually accompanied by diarrhoea and vomiting. To the modern doctor colic might be any one of a number of disorders, but the doctor in the early years of our period did not differentiate. Paregoric at that time was the usual prescription for colic. Paregoric, being the camphorated tincture of opium, usually soothed the pain, but was no cure for the disease. Towards the end of the period, however, the treatment for colic became much more scientific.

Appendicitis in the nineties was diagnosed as "inflammation of the bowels", and was treated with castor oil, hot compresses on the stomach, and sometimes hot irons to the soles of the feet. Later an operation was substituted for palliatives. When the doctors discovered how easily this operation could be performed, they really went to town. A pain in your tummy from eating too many green apples, and out came your appendix. You were lucky to reach thirty without a scar on your abdomen. The fee for an appendectomy was $25.

A ruptured appendix was a different matter. It was usually fatal until Dr. Grove of Fergus experimented with the technique of flushing the abdominal cavity with an antiseptic solution after an operation to prevent peritonitis.

Dr. Grove was a resourceful and skillful physician of the old school. He established an excellent hospital, and administered it with such efficiency that it actually made a small profit. One day I sat talking to Dr. Grove on his verandah, when he pointed to a young woman who waved to him as she walked past.

"See that woman? " he said.

"Yes," I said.

"I brought her into the world on the dining-room table of a farm-house. I was caught short in an acute emergency with no anesthetic and no surgical instruments. I performed a Caesarean section with a well sharpened carving knife from the kitchen."

Dr. Grove was a good, old-fashioned doctor, who would do his best whatever the circumstances.

During the period under study almost every family was touched in one way or another with tuberculosis, then called consumption. The highly contagious character of the disease was not fully realized in the nineties, and no effective treatment was known. A "change of climate" was often recommended. Alexander Graham Bell, who was threatened with consumption, and his parents left Scotland and migrated to Canada in search of a change of climate. Early in the twentieth century sanitariums became popular, and patients were made to live and sleep outdoors on spacious verandahs summer or winter, fair weather or foul. Those who survived the rigors of the treatment, were usually able to resist the further onslaughts of the disease. At one time garlic was considered to be beneficial in the treatment of tuberculosis, and the corridors of the sanitarium at Gravenhurst reeked with the odor of this pungent herb.

A.M.

House call

On the afternoon of November 8, 1895, Wilhelm Conrad
Roentgen was carrying out routine experiments with a Crookes
tube at Wuertemberg University in Germany. He was investigat-
ing cathode rays. A Crookes tube was made by sealing two
electrodes (one positive, one negative) into a glass bulb and then
removing most of the air from the bulb. For his purpose he had
completely darkened the room and had encased the bulb in
light-proof cardboard. When everything was ready, he activated
the tube by turning on the current.

He became aware immediately that something strange was
happening. A curious luminosity had appeared on a nearby
bench. When he lit a match to investigate, he found that by
chance a barium platinocyanide screen had been left lying on
the bench. The strange gleam had been produced by some form
of invisible radiation escaping from the tube and striking this
fluorescent screen. He repeated the operation several times,
always with the same result. What type of radiation could be
involved? It could not be cathode rays, because cathode rays
do not readily penetrate glass; it could not be light rays, because
light rays do not penetrate cardboard. With considerable excitement, he realized that he was dealing with some phenomenon

new to science. To indicate that, except for their ability to penetrate cardboard, the properties of the mysterious rays were as yet unknown, he called them X-strahlen, or X-rays.

Thus by accident he had hit on one of the most astounding, the most revolutionary discoveries ever made in the science of medicine.

All over the civilized world scientists took to experimenting with what were soon dubbed Roentgen rays. Quickly it was found out that these electromagnetic rays would penetrate human tissue, but not more solid substances such as bone. Less than three months after Roentgen made his discovery, a Canadian scientist used X-rays for diagnostic purposes. A young man had been shot in the leg. Doctors had probed without success for the bullet, and the wound had been allowed to heal. When the bullet began to trouble the young man, John Cox, a physicist on the staff of McGill University in Montreal, undertook to locate it by X-ray.

A chair was placed on a table, and the youth was required to sit on the chair. A photographic plate was held against his leg by a heavy block of wood. To prevent movement the plate and the block were bound tightly to the leg by bandages and towels. For forty-five minutes the leg was exposed to rays from the vacuum tube. When the photographic plate was developed, a vague shadow close to the bone indicated the location of the bullet. To remove it, all that was required was a simple operation.

Manufacturers quickly saw their opportunity and began producing X-ray machines. Progressive doctors had these primitive machines installed in their offices. At first the apparatus was used mainly to locate bone fractures, or to detect foreign substances in the human body — buttons or safety-pins that a child had swallowed, or bullets or shreds of metal in the bodies of older people.

Enterprising doctors, however, were eager to extend the use of the machine to the exploration of the gastrointestinal system. There was, however, one difficulty. The stomach, the duodenum, and the intestines were not dense enough to produce a readily discernible shadow on the photographic plate. Bismuth compounds were at the time being prescribed in the treatment of gastric ulcers, and, since bismuth is opaque to X-rays, it offered itself as a "contrast medium". Bismuth mixed with liquid food was therefore fed to patients, and its progress through the digestive system was recorded on photographic plates. After much practice doctors were able to recognize the shadowy indications of ulcers, malignancies, and other abnormalities. Today other substances including barium sulphate are substituted for the traditional "bismuth meal".

It had become apparent as early as 1908 that the proper operation of X-ray apparatus had become too complicated and too time-consuming for the busy general practitioner, and a new specialist emerged — the radiologist. By the time the First World War broke out every hospital had an X-ray department operated by trained technicians and supervised by a doctor who was usually a specialist in radiology.

* * *

The interesting thing, however, is not the doctor of the period, who with his limited knowledge (limited at least by modern standards) achieved marvels, but the home remedies in general use.

Sir William Osler's mother, for instance, always insisted that the cure for a cold was to immerse the patient's feet in a bath of hot whisky. But the more common cure was a mustard bath for the feet and goose grease and turpentine for the chest. Often a red flannel cloth or better still a sweaty sock was wound around the throat. Aspirin was, of course, unknown.

If a person suffered a severe cut, one of the popular methods of preventing infection was to sprinkle the wound thoroughly with black pepper. If this drastic treatment did not work and the wound festered, the best way to draw out the poison was to apply a bread poultice. If the case was a particularly stubborn one, a poultice of soap and sugar might be used. Such a poultice would be painful, but it would do the job.

Mustard plasters were extensively used. If you had a pain in your belly a mustard plaster was slapped on; if you had a cough on your chest, a mustard plaster was applied; if you had an ache in your head — well, in that case the mustard was applied to the feet. Why, I don't know. But it worked.

There was a dentist who lived in Sudbury. Every year he came down to Toronto to the dental convention. And every year he ate too much, and he drank too much, with the result that he developed a bad pain in his tummy from indigestion. When he was approaching thirty, he decided that it was time to take a wife. He looked around, found a suitable woman and in due course they were married.

The first year of their marriage she came down to the convention with him. But in spite of everything she could do he ate too much, and he drank too much. They took the overnight train back to Sudbury. And sure enough at two o'clock in the morning he began to groan.

"Oh! my poor stomach. Oh! Oh! Oh! What a pain I have! "

Dutifully his wife got out of the berth, opened the suitcase, and found the makings of a mustard plaster. Sleepily she staggered to the end of the coach, but the only water she could find was the ice water for drinking.

With the ice-cold mustard plaster in her hand, she found her way back to the berth, opened the curtain, pulled down the blanket, yanked up the pyjamas, and slapped the ice-cold plaster on the bare belly.

To her dismay a voice she had never heard before said, "Jesus Christ! "

Tonics of one sort or another were much prized at the turn of the century.

Nowadays tonics have to be pushed over the counter by hard--sell commercials on television. But the old method of increasing sales was much simpler and much subtler. Almost all the tonics had a high alcoholic content. Beef, Iron, and Wine (is it still obtainable today?) though its alcoholic content was comparatively low, was one of the most popular. You could get a large bottle for 20c, and if you gave the druggist 5c more, he would mix in a quantity of quinine. The bitter quinine spoiled the taste, but apparently it made the tonic more effective.

Without the quinine, Beef, Iron, and Wine was a pleasant-tasting cordial. And if you drank enough of it — well, here is a true story.

In the head office of a well known insurance company quite often a fair amount of money was kept overnight in a safe in the manager's office. One night the policeman on the beat observed a light in the manager's office, where no light should have been. He phoned headquarters and waited. Headquarters sent reinforcements and called the manager. When the manager arrived on the scene with the keys, three policemen and the manager entered the building. Other policemen arranged themselves so that they could watch both the front and the back entrances.

Convinced that they were going to surprise a safe-cracker at his nefarious work, the four men inside the building stealthily ascended to the third floor, where the manager's office was situated. When they were assembled outside the office, the policemen drew their revolvers and burst open the door.

But what they discovered was no safe-cracker. It was only the night watchman blissfully asleep in the middle of the carpeted floor. He was surrounded by twenty-four empty bottles labelled Beef, Iron, and Wine. Where he had succeeded in getting hold of a whole case of the cordial nobody ever found out. And it is even more of a mystery how he managed to dispose of the contents of so many bottles.

A rival to Beef, Iron, and Wine in popularity was Peruna. It was excellent for almost anything that ailed you. Its alcoholic content was higher than most of our fortified wines today, and just about on a par with our debilitated whisky. And you could drink it with a free conscience even if you were a prominent church worker. Who could blame you for taking a dose of medicine? Or even three or four doses? Ultimately the "Peruna jag" became such a scandal that this and other delightful concoctions were outlawed by a kill-joy government.

Sulphur and molasses was given to children in the spring. This curious mixture was supposed to "purify the blood", getting rid of poisons accumulated during the winter. A loathsome concoction to swallow, it was dreaded by all children. But its repulsive taste was supposed to contribute to its beneficial effects. My grandfather firmly believed that a medicine to do you any good had to be obnoxious. The belief that one could attain moral or physical health by torturing oneself, typically medieval, was still strong at the turn of the century.

Beef tea, made by boiling beef and adding salt and pepper to taste, was considered to be highly nutritious, and was given in quantity to convalescents. It is no longer popular, however, partly because with the multiplicity of canned consommées now available housewives are too lazy to make it, and partly because doctors have come to doubt its special nutritive value. It is a different story with raw beef sandwiches. You made the filling for these sandwiches by scraping raw beef, a tedious process. In spite of the fact that they are not only pleasant to eat but highly nutritious, raw beef sandwiches are no longer popular, no doubt because you can't find scraped beef in the frozen-food counter at the supermarket.

One of the curious superstitions of the period was the belief that the smell of a gas works would help to cure whooping cough. Superstition always steps in, where science has failed. At the time, there was no real cure for whooping cough.

There were those, of course, who took advantage of ignorant people's fears and gullibility. Every so often some shyster, often disguised as an Indian, would set up his stand in the market place and would do a roaring trade selling his magical nostrum, "good for man or beast". One enterprising salesman carried with him a jar containing two or three tape-worms, which he displayed on his stand before launching on his spiel. If you listened to him for ten minutes, and looked long enough at his revolting sales gimmick, you would gladly pay a dollar for a bottle of the medicine, which was guaranteed to free your intestines of such loathsome parasites.

With the increased use of electricity in the home came many marvelous electrical remedies. Electricity was the great mystery of the age, the one thing that even scientists could not understand. Its power was magical. It could run streetcars, light homes, and carry the human voice over miles of copper wire. Was there anything it could not do? Knowing very little about it, people were ready to believe that it was capable of performing miracles. They were just as gullible then as they are now. One of the most popular health-giving gadgets was an electric belt, which you wore next your skin. No electricity whatever was involved. But in the advertisements was the picture of a muscular man wearing one of the belts, and you could see the health-giving beams of electricity radiating out in all directions. Thousands of the belts were sold, and many people who bought them were willing to swear that they were highly beneficial.

Ill-informed doctors of today believe that the electric shock treatment is a comparatively modern discovery. What nonsense! It was in common use seventy years ago. To be sure it was used, not for mental illness, but for general debility. The current was produced by a box-like contraption with two wires which ended in grips for the hands. When you took hold of the grips, one in each hand, and the machine was turned on you received a mild shock. The fact that the current went right through you from one hand to the other was supposed to be very beneficial. If you held one grip and your best girl held the other, and then you joined hands, the salubrious effect of the shock was almost doubled.

A prized item in every household was the Doctor's Book. It was the popular do-it-yourself hand-book of the period. It described every common complaint, its symptoms and its cure. Jerome K. Jerome, who wrote "Three Men in a Boat", consulted a Doctor's Book and discovered by checking the symptoms that he had every disease in the book except housemaid's knee. The pictures in the book were something to marvel at. They depicted all the organs of the body in sickness and in health. The picture of a degenerated human heart, bloated and destroyed from drinking too much alcohol, was enough to frighten any drunkard out of his besotted senses.

Though the doctors of the period were usually wise and competent, they also had their fads. In the early years of this century one of these medical fads was the rest cure. If you were a bit under par, complaining of this and that, but evidencing no sign of serious disease, the doctor would decide that what you needed was the rest cure. He would send you to the hospital, where the nurses knew exactly what to do with you. They would put you to bed and feed you several times a day with the richest types of food — eggnogs, raw eggs by the dozen, puddings drowned in thick cream, and other foods high in calories. Your friends sent you boxes of chocolates, which you consumed at will; and your relatives brought you cream puffs and custard pies. For three or four weeks you did nothing but eat and sleep. When you came out of the hospital you were completely relaxed and plumper by some twenty or thirty pounds. You looked, in fact, exactly like one of Swift's butterball turkeys, cleaned and plucked and ready for the oven.

How appallingly different things are today! Nowadays the nurses, heartless creatures, get you out of bed at the earliest possible moment, even after a serious operation. And the modern doctor seems to have an unfeeling prejudice against a pot-bellied patient. Reducing diets are the thing today.

* * *

The parlor in the house of the period was used mainly for company. But it had another function a bit more sombre. When all known home remedies had been employed in vain, and when the doctor had applied his best skill but to no avail, and the poor patient had died, he was laid out in a simple coffin in the parlor, and the whole household went into mourning. A crepe was hung on the front door, the women dressed in black with heavy black veils hanging from their black bonnets, and the men wore black arm-bands on their sleeves. It was customary for the members of the family to continue in mourning for six months, sometimes for a year. It was not unknown for a woman who had lost her husband to continue in mourning for the rest of her life.

The funeral service was an impressive ceremony. Sometimes the preacher held forth for almost an hour on the virtues of the deceased (even when these were non-existent) and dwelt with satisfaction on the glories of everlasting life among the angels (even when a stern theology would seem to consign the departed soul to hell).

Death was a serious business in those years. People were not made callous by daily reports of traffic accidents on our streets and highways. Today we just raise an eyebrow and say "Too bad! " when a whole family of six is wiped out in one appalling holocaust of flaming gasolene and twisted steel.

The time when the body lay in state in the parlor was a time of great strain on members of the household. Friends and relatives came from far and near, and all comers had to be provided with food, chicken and ham with all the trimmings, and of course drink. Many of the visitors would not think that they had properly honored the deceased unless they became slightly tipsy – unless, of course, the household was strictly teetotal.

A FAMILY CHRISTMAS
by Margaret H. Wilton

It was a week before Christmas. Already a spirit of restless-ness pervaded the house — a restlessness approaching excite-ment. Every ring at the door-bell, every sleigh-bell on the street, every bell pealing across the winter night from the Anglican church at the corner, suggested something imminent. Ex-pectation filled our minutes.

Daily the excitement grew. My two sisters and I had not known many Christmases, but memories were indelible. Now it was here again — that wonderful time. It was 1910 and I was eight years old. Each day held delight, each day brought us nearer to that time, which was uppermost in our thoughts. Everything seemed special; smells from the kitchen, mysterious parcels coming to the house and disappearing, lots of mail each time the postman came, and soft snow falling silently outdoors. All were part of the mystery.

Suddenly we remembered that the parcels from New Brunswick would come any time now. Our mother had come from New Brunswick, and every Christmas the express man brought to our door two big boxes from Fredericton. They had always arrived early, so back and forth we ran to the front window looking hopefully up the street for the big red express wagon. Sometimes both of us carried a stool from the kitchen and pulling aside the parlour curtains, placed the stool right at the glass. From this vantage point we took turns keeping watch and chanting, "Express man, express man, where are you? " Oh, what was that? Something was coming down the street. Now we saw it, now the horses turned in towards the sidewalk and stopped in front of our house. This was the moment we had waited for. We all ran to the door, the one then on the stool knocking it over in her haste. The driver smiled and handed us the boxes. Both had reached Kingston that day. They were large, wrapped in brown paper, with lots of stickers and the address in large letters. Yes, they were ours. Just then, Mother came down the hall. "Take these into the dining room," she said. They were always put in there on a table behind the door and we knew that they would be kept there until Christmas Eve. These boxes were always opened on Christmas Eve. Still, we could look at them and wonder what we would find inside. Then when the time came, we would find out.

Wondering led to action. We knew we must not open the boxes, but perhaps we could stick our fingers in the corners and feel inside. That was easy. By tearing the wrapping at a corner and taking turns poking first with one finger and then with two, we soon had a hole big enough to put a hand in. We couldn't see much, but we could feel; small square parcels — maybe a ring; longer flat ones, quite large — probably a tie, or maybe socks, for father; other large flat ones — perhaps towels or pillow slips for mother. We knew that in the bottom of one box — the one from Aunt Martha's home — there would be two large parcels, one containing doughnuts and the other short-bread, made by Aunt Serene, an elderly relative who lived there, and could she cook!

We checked the boxes at intervals to feel those parcels and anticipate the probable contents. Soon it would be time to decorate the tree. It was two days before Christmas now. The previous night father had dragged a beautiful evergreen through the snow from the nearby grocery store and fastened it to two slabs of wood set on the floor at right angles. It stood in the corner of the parlour, its tip almost touching the ceiling. Its fragrance filled the room. We could hardly wait to start decorating it.

We couldn't decorate it until we had the decorations ready. Some were kept from year to year in a large box in a cupboard in the upper hall. Mother brought the box downstairs and we opened it. There were long ropes of tinsel, coloured ornaments to fasten on the tips of the branches, and a big shiny star to be put at the very top of the tree. Just looking at them brought excitement. But we had to have chains of popcorn, so as soon as supper was over and we had washed the dishes and father had checked the furnace and the kitchen stove, a bottle of pop-corn kernels was brought out from the back of the kitchen cupboard. Then father brought the shaker from the back kitchen. How we shivered with excitement. The shaker was a heavy wire cage, about 5" by 5" by 4" deep, fastened on the end of a 4' handle. The lid of the cage opened and shut with a hook. Father opened the lid and sprinkled a thick layer of the kernels on the bottom of the cage, and then fastened the lid again. We could hardly wait. Opening the long narrow door in the front of the stove, where fresh coal was put in, father looked in to see the flames. Still we had to wait. When the flames had died down, leaving only hot coals, the fun began. We took turns holding the long handle so that the cage was over the hot coals, and shaking the cage vigorously. Pop-pop, each little kernel exploded into a sort of bumpy white ball; pop-pop-pop — till the cage was full. Taking it out, we flipped back the lid and emptied the lovely white 'pop-corn' into a big bowl. Then more kernels were put in the little cage and more pop-corn appeared. This was repeated several times until we knew we had enough to make our pop-corn chains the next day.

The next day — the day before Christmas — we were up early. That tree was to be decorated and we had work to do first. Breakfast dishes were washed and dried with dangerous speed, rooms were tidied and dusted. Mother remembered one or two things she needed from a little store a few blocks away. We could not send for anything as we did not have a telephone, so I went as fast as I could and got them. I remember that little store well. The family lived in the back part and prepared the food, which customers bought in the front section. One wonderful item was a raisin pie with delicious crust and plump juicy raisins. It cost 10 cents.

Before dinner, we made the chains. The big bowl of pop-corn was placed on the kitchen table. I sat on the kitchen stool in front of the table and my sisters on the bench, which was behind it. Two of us always sat there at meals. To get to our dining-room you had to go half-way down the hall leading to the front of the house, so except on special occasions or when we had company, we ate in the kitchen. Now we were ready. Each had a needle, quite fine so it wouldn't break the pop-corn; we threaded these with long white threads, 6 or 8 feet in length, and put a knot at the end. Then holding a piece of pop-corn

Christmas eve

in our left hand we gently pushed the needle through it with our right hand and then carefully pulled the piece of pop-corn to the end of the thread. Again and again we did this until we had a long chain of lovely white balls. When all the pop-corn had been threaded, we took all the chains and put them with the other decorations and then put the large box in the parlour beside the tree, which was waiting.

Now it was afternoon and time to put the tree in fancy dress. What fun! We all worked at once. We took turns standing on a stool and twisting chains of tinsel and pop-corn around the lovely green branches. Then we fastened the little ornaments to the end of some of the branches. We left the large star, which was to be at the very top, for father to put up when he came home from work. The tree stood there filling the room with beauty. Mother came in and said, "Oh, how lovely! " Some people always fastened little candles on the ends of the branches. When they were lighted, the tree looked wonderful, but mother and father knew that this was a dangerous thing to do, so we were never allowed to use candles. When father came home he brought in a small step-ladder and climbing up, put the large star at the very top. Now, it was done.

That night was to hold more excitement so supper was quickly over and the dishes washed. Again the stove and the furnace had to be checked. Then — how exciting it was now! The two big boxes which the express man had brought a few days before were carried from the dining room and placed on the kitchen table. We three perched on the table beside them. Mother sat on a chair and father stood. Then he took each box in turn, untied the cord, took off the brown paper and opened the top. There were the parcels in tissue-paper, tied with coloured ribbon and decorated with Christmas stickers and tags with names on them. He read a name and then handed the parcel to the person mentioned. We all watched while each parcel was opened. Squeals of delight filled the room. The parcels of doughnuts and shortbread came last and were left in the kitchen, while we took our opened presents to the parlour and put them under the tree.

There was a ring at the door bell. My older sister ran to the door. Two aunts — sisters of my father — were there, and they had parcels. We didn't open those; they also went under the tree, but they would be opened in the morning. Mother went to the kitchen and got a doughnut and a piece of shortbread for each. This was a regular custom. Shortly after they left there were two rings of the bell. We knew that was a lady from across the street. She always rang twice. She too always came on Christmas Eve for her Christmas treat.

Soon it was bed time. We looked out the window at the sky. Stars were shining. Up at the corner a Salvation Army band was playing "Silent Night, Holy Night". There was something wonderful about it all. We took a last look at the tree in the parlour, glittering in the lamplight. Then the light went out and the door was shut. Now there was one more thing to do. Mother handed each of us a black stocking and father hung them from the mantel in the dining room. Then the three of us were sent to bed. We weren't a bit sleepy, but we had to go. We knew that things would be happening downstairs once we were out of the way.

Sleep came slowly. Gradually the street sounds — the voices, the sleigh-bells and the laughter — lessened. Downstairs seemed farther away and then came the silence of dreamland. But it was a broken dreamland. I wakened several times. All was quiet and dark. Once I pulled the window curtain back and looked at the sky. The stars seemed specially bright. I knew it was not yet morning so I got into bed again and tried to go to sleep, but sleep eluded me. Long before it was light a voice came from the room where my younger sister slept. "Is it time to get up? " and from my parent's room, "No, it is not morning yet. Go back to sleep." This happened several times until finally — in desperation I guess — my father got up. Immediately three little girls were out of bed. In our flannelette nighties we rushed to the top of the stairs. Father lit a lamp and clad in his night-shirt, and holding the lamp in his right hand, he started down the stairs. We followed, almost stumbling in our eagerness. The dining-room door was opened and in the lamplight we saw the three stockings, huge the night before, now bulging and bumpy, each with a candy cane sticking out the top. A name was fastened to each stocking so we could claim our own. Back we went up the stairs holding our precious stockings. Sitting on top of our beds we took out the contents — there was the candy cane at the top, and an orange filling the toe — there were lovely big walnuts waiting to be cracked. A number of little bumpy parcels each contained a candy animal; a dog, a bird, a horse, a cat, all made of sugar candy. Then each stocking held another gift. I found one very small parcel and in it a gold ring. At least it looked like gold. It was my first ring. Already my day was made.

It was still early, but who could go back to sleep now ! Everyone dressed and went downstairs. The parlour door was shut and we knew we had to have breakfast before that door would be opened. Again stove and furnace had to be tended. On that morning it seemed to us that father spent an extra long time doing this job. Then the porridge, which had been made the night before and left in a pot on the back of the stove to keep warm, had to be stirred thoroughly. Then we had to eat and who wanted porridge and toast and milk that day!

Finally the big moment came. We had finished breakfast and tidied the kitchen and then here we were outside the parlour door. Father opened the door. All was dark and mysterious. Suddenly a lamp was lighted. There was the tree as we had left it, but now, underneath, and tucked among its branches, were parcels not there the night before. It didn't take us long to find our own. I still remember my "Eaton's Beauty" doll. I think

I carried it with me all day. It was quite a large doll with curly hair. Eaton's was famous at that time for those dolls. Every little girl wanted one.

It took a while to pick up the wrappings and ribbons which had been strewn around the floor, and then over and over we looked at all the presents: candy, skates, woollen scarves — in those days called 'clouds' — beads, woollen toques, games, and other lovely things. We sat there excited and happy until almost noon. Postmen came often in those days and when one arrived on that Christmas morning, the three of us rushed to the door and came back with our hands full of envelopes. What fun to hear from people in all parts of the country!

Soon it was afternoon. For a little while we played on the college hill — we lived near Queen's University and its grounds had always been our playground. Bundled up in our winter coats and toques, overstockings, mittens and clouds, we went out and across the street into the college grounds pulling a sled behind us. Father came too. He didn't have many holidays, and getting out in the snow that afternoon was a treat. The evergreens at the top of the hill were heavy with snow; the sky was blue with white clouds drifting across. There were a lot of people over there, children and adults, and we could hear laughter and shouting as we walked under the trees. We took turns having a ride. Sometimes two of us got on the sled. Father gave us a push and down we went to the bottom. Then we pulled the sled up the hill again. The fathers were enjoying it as much as the children.

We didn't stay too long because that night was a big occasion. We were going to my grandma's home for Christmas dinner. Dinner was at night on Christmas. My father had three sisters there. Then another sister and her husband and three sons were coming, and we knew we would have a good time. First we had to put on our Sunday dresses and our new hair-ribbons. Father polished our boots until they shone. I wore my new ring, and my doll — the "Eaton's Beauty" — went too. Mother wore a heavy coat and a velvet hat, and she had a round fur muff to keep her hands warm. We walked the seven or eight blocks we had to go; my sisters and I having turns being pulled on a sled by my father. The street-cars didn't run on Sundays or holidays.

Christmas dinner

There were no taxis; the automobile hadn't yet appeared on the streets. Some people had a cutter drawn by horses. These people were sitting covered with buffalo robes as their cutters passed us, the sleigh-bells jingling as the horses pranced through the snow. Now we were there. The door opened. Is there anything more memorable than a Christmas night, a door opening into a lighted house, and from the kitchen, delicious smells of turkey and vegetables, plum pudding and Christmas cake? We could hardly wait to sit around the table.

All too soon the evening ended. The Christmas dinner was over; we had stopped playing in the parlour with some of our presents, which we had brought up with us, and we were getting sleepy. It had been a long day and an exciting day. Now it was time to go home. We were quieter now, and when we got home were quite willing to go to bed, only we had to have one more look at the tree. We opened our parlour door. A lamp was lit. There it was, glittering and beautiful — such a picture as would remain in memory long after childhood had passed.

Christmas is very different now. The simple joys: sleigh bells jingling on the snowy streets, Christmas carols sung in the parlour; children drawn on sleds to the nearest hill, and skating on the ice in the back yard, and walking to their grandma's for Christmas dinner — all these things have partly given way in places, especially larger centres, to something resembling a commercial carnival: many houses almost hidden by costly lights, the owners trying to outdo their neighbours, carols mechanically produced in stores and even on subway platforms — more noise than music; crowds rushing in and out of stores on last minute shopping sprees; the shoppers tired and cross, the clerks exhausted, noisy Christmas Eve parties and noisy streets. And yet, still on Christmas Eve a few churches hold midnight service and in that mystic atmosphere our thoughts go back to long ago, and we relive a childhood Christmas, and it seems that from far above the city's racket there comes a song:

> Glory to God in the highest,
> And on earth peace to men of good will.

ENTERTAINMENT

by Adrian Macdonald

It is hard for young people today, when many youngsters carry a transistor radio in their pockets, to imagine a time when it was necessary for people to provide most of their own entertainment.

At any rate, in those distant days we were not blase. Music was a treat, not a necessary concomitant of all our waking hours. Nowadays we turn on the radio as soon as we enter a room, not because we wish especially to hear what is being broadcast, but because we want a rackety shield against the irksome insistence of silence. We are afraid of being alone with our thoughts. We feel uncomfortable, if our ears are not being assailed by the persistent beat of rock-and-roll orchestras or the crooning or yelling of popular singers. Our taste is so blunted by a surfeit of rhythmic clamor that, if we are not thoroughly addicted to the classics, we crave nothing but the insistent drumming of frenetic teen-age dance music — one, two, three, four; one, two, three, four; the old Bach beat, titivated up to please the modern fancy.

So redundant is the mechanical production of music, that we are in danger of becoming bored even with the classics. How often have we heard Chopin's better known piano pieces, Tchaikovsky's "Nutcracker Suite", or Beethoven's symphonies? Even Christmas carols, which were once so lovely, have become nothing but a crashing bore. No wonder modern composers are vying with each other in their search for far-out novelty — for new and strange sounds, complicated variations of rhythm, acrid dissonances.

When we were young things were very different. Occasionally a well known musician would visit our town and put on a concert at the local theatre. In this way I heard two or three famous violinists, a cellist (whose name I have forgotten, but whose playing I still vividly remember) and Paderewski. As soon as Paderewski stepped out on the stage you knew that he was either a famous magician like Houdini, or a real musician. His long beautifully waved auburn hair, his aristocratic features, and his dignified manner fired your imagination before he ever sat down at the piano.

It was in this way also that I heard Jessie McLaughlin who sang Scottish songs with great éclat. It was rumored, with what truth I do not know, that Jessie was devoted not only to Scotland's songs but to Scotland's famous beverage. But a little weakness of that sort in no way affected our admiration for her singing. John McCormack, the famous Irish tenor, I did not hear until much later, and then only on records.

At Christmas time the church choir would put on a cantata or a concert of Christmas carols. When I was at high school the choir of a downtown church gave a public performance of "The Messiah". For me it was a soul-shaking experience. Never before had I heard anything like it. The floods of melody, the ebb and flow of pulsating sound, the resounding climaxes swept away all triviality, all meanness, and revealed to me in a magnificent vision all the glory and the sorrow of life and death and eternity.

At about the same time too, I had my first experience of Beethoven. A friend who had a phonograph bought a recording of the adagio movement of Beethoven's Sonata in C minor Opus 13. I played the record over and over until he must have felt like breaking it over my head. I was so impressed with the grandeur of this music, that I taught myself to play the piano, not well by conservatory standards, but well enough to play two or three of Beethoven's sonatas passably.

Ambitious amateur groups, after a good deal of rehearsing, sometimes performed a Gilbert and Sullivan opera. My wife remembers an occasion when the choir boys of the church, with the help of certain girls from the congregation, put on "Pinafore". But choir boys couldn't of course be permitted to say damn, so they sang instead:

"Did you hear him? Don't go near him;
He is swearing. He said hang it, he said hang it."

The audience knew the little devils who were pretending to be so prim, and let out such a roar of laughter that it was almost impossible for them to finish the performance.

Most towns of any size had a band, sometimes a regimental band, which headed all parades and sometimes gave concerts in the park. Often even villages had bands of a sort, which made up in enthusiasm what they lacked in musicianship.

Ralph, who was seven years old at the time, remembers very vividly a village band at a political rally in 1911. He had four brothers and sisters, and they were brought up on a farm near Port Perry. On this particular day early in June, along with their mother and father, they all climbed into the democrat, and behind a shining team of standard-bred horses they drove into the village. From a mile away on the still air they could hear the band playing "The Maple Leaf" and "Rule Britannia" with resounding enthusiasm. When they got to the picnic grounds Ralph immediately sought out the band. But what impressed him was not their music, but their head-gear. They all wore white caps with black peaks. And Ralph thought that the most marvelous thing in life would be the right to wear one of those caps. There were trotting races on the village racetrack, followed by a race between Tom Longboat, an Indian, and Alfie Shrubb, an Englishman, two famous runners of the day. Robert Borden, the Conservative leader, made a speech, but Ralph didn't think much of him. He didn't wear a white cap with a shiny black peak. Then the band marched about the field playing "The Girl I Left Behind Me", "The British Grenadiers", and other martial airs.

But so far as he can remember, Ralph (for many years he has been a dentist) never in his life got to wear one of those white caps.

Now every home has a hi-fi phonograph, one or two portable radios, and a television set, all requiring merely to be turned on. When we were young you didn't turn on music. You produced it. Every home had a piano or an organ. If there were youngsters in the home one of them was certain to be given piano lessons. Very few turned out to be accomplished musicians, but some at least learned to thump their way through a dance tune, or provide a few chords as accompaniment for a sentimental song.

We produced music

Anyone who could play the piano for dancing was in demand. My wife's Aunt Sarah was master of only one piece. "Oh dear! What can the Matter Be? ", but she was always willing to oblige. When a dance was to be held a large canvas was rented and spread over the parlor carpet like a tarpaulin over a football field today. When this canvas was waxed it made an excellent surface for dancing. And Aunt Sarah would play her piece over and over again — ONE, two, three; ONE, two, three. She came down on the accented note as if she were pounding a bass drum. But nobody objected. Boys who were just learning to waltz found the heavy accent helped them to untangle their awkward feet. When the company wished to dance a polka or a two-step, some abler pianist than Aunt Sarah had to be called upon. The tango came in not long before the outbreak of the First World War. A girl from Chicago tried to teach us how to dance it, I am afraid without much success.

In the country the musician was usually a fiddler, and the favorite dance was the square dance, still popular today.

To the teen-agers of today our repertory of dances undoubtedly seems very old-fashioned. But believe me we really danced. A polka, for instance, was a romp, a frolic; and a waltz with the lights turned low and a pretty partner in your arms was a romantic experience to cherish among your souvenirs. The solemn and silly mating rituals which youngsters indulge in today, where they do not execute a single dance step, but just imitate the prancing and wiggling of primitive tribes, seem to us merely ridiculous.

The popular songs of the period were sentimental ditties like "In the Shade of the Old Apple Tree", and "I Wonder Who's Kissing Her Now". But some of the music was more stirring. Rag-time, the old-fashioned progenitor of jazz, was very popular. And in 1892 Lottie Collins, dressed in a scarlet skirt, introduced in a London music hall the rollicking ballad, Ta-ra-ra-boom-de-ay, and for many years it rocked the whole civilized world. Everybody sang it. A generation later, in 1914 when the British Expeditionary Force arrived in France they were welcomed by French youngsters singing the song under the impression that it was the British national anthem.

For amusement in our reading we had at our disposal the great Victorian novelists (by Jove! how those old boys could tell a story!) and short story writers like Conan Doyle, Rudyard Kipling, and Jerome K. Jerome. What has happened to the short story today? Has it been displaced by the mysteries and the sitcoms on television? For boys there were the Henty books, which were fascinating historical yarns, and for girls the Elsie books (God forgive our girls for reading such trash!). Ralph Connor was the most popular Canadian novelist of the period. Ralph Connor was the pen name of a Presbyterian minister in Winnipeg, whose real name was Dr. Charles Gordon. He embodied Canadian life in such powerful novels as "Glengarry School Days" and "Sky Pilot". L. M. Montgomery, the wife of a Presbyterian minister in Prince Edward Island, also wrote many truly Canadian novels, the most famous of which was "Anne of Green Gables". Then, of course, there was Nellie McClung, who published "Sowing Seeds in Danny" in 1908, and followed it with several other best-selling novels. But Nellie McClung is so important in other ways than as a novelist that we are including elsewhere a separate account of her personality and her work.

Much of the poetry of the period had a note rarely found in modern poetry, a touch of sweet, old-fashioned sentimentality. James Whitcome Riley was an American poet who was born in Greenfield, Indiana. He was not a great poet like Tennyson, but he was immensely popular at the turn of the century. The titles of two of his books, "To an Old Sweetheart of Mine" and "Old Fashioned Roses", suggest the fragrance of his verses. They were tenderly sentimental. To a great many of us such heart warming sentiment will always have a strong appeal. Why has it disappeared? Are poets today afraid of being just ordinary folk? What is needed is a modern Wordsworth to drag poetry away from the esoteric region of far-out experimentation and restore it to its proper function of dealing with the joys and sorrows of everyday life.

* * *

As an example of the sort of entertainment available in theatres in the mid-nineties, I offer the following advertisement from the St. Thomas Daily Times:

"Sept. 10, 11 and 12
The Townsend Shakespearean Co. will appear
in their charming repertoire of selections from
Shakespearean Plays, Standard Comedies and
laughable Farces. An entertainment both amusing and intellectual, and free from any feature
that the most fastidious could object to."

Whew! Imagine such an advertisement appearing in a news-paper today when even the least fastidious gasp at some of the raw sexuality in plays and movies!

It was in the Duncombe Opera House (the theatre in which the Townsend company appeared) that I attended my first play. It was a performance of "Uncle Tom's Cabin". I was just six years old at the time, and my uncle, with whom I was going to the play, first took me down to Talbot Street to see the parade which the company of actors put on to publicise their per-formance. The parade was headed by a band which, in spite of its diminutive size, made a tremendous racket. There were Negroes in the procession, the first that I had ever seen. Uncle Tom with his snowy-white woolly hair was particularly striking. Little Eva, very pretty and very demure, ambled along on a white pony. And of course Topsy, and Miss Ophelia, and the cruel slave owner, Simon Legree, who carried a vicious-looking whip which he cracked ominously. But it was the bloodhounds which most fascinated me. Like most big dogs they were probably very good-tempered. But as I watched them straining at their leashes I was sure that they would tear to pieces anyone they could pounce on.

Before we entered the theatre my uncle bought me a bag of globe chocolates, but by the time we had shoved through the crowd to our seats in the balcony the chocolates were crushed into a mass as flat as a pancake. In my young mind the tragedy of the chocolates was at least as grave as the tragedy of little Eva in the play.

Going up to Heaven

My memories of the play are confined to three or four scenes which shimmer vaguely before my inner vision like dissolving pictures on a television screen. Simon Legree, the bad guy, beating poor Uncle Tom with his ugly whip; Topsy, with her hair done up in pigtails all over her head, telling Miss Ophelia, the prim New England spinster, that she hadn't been born, she just growed; Eliza fleeing across the river on floating blocks of ice, with the bloodhounds baying behind her on the river bank; and little Eva, wiggling pathetically like a worm on a fish-hook, being dragged up to heaven at the end of a clothes-line.

The most famous of all the touring companies seventy years ago was the Marks Brothers. (Not of course the famous Marx Brothers. They came much later when movies became popular). Tom Marks was the oldest brother and took most of the principal parts. For several years they toured the province, putting on plays in theatres, Masonic halls, even in barns with considerable success. Their repertory consisted mostly of thrilling melodramas. There would be a scene depicting a lighthouse on a stormy night, and the lighthouse keeper's wife would say in a deep throaty voice, "God have mercy on the poor souls at sea tonight! " Or a scene in which the righteously indignant father would drive his erring daughter out of the house on a wintry night with a shawl over her head and her illegitimate chee-ild in her arms. She would of course return in the last act of the play, when her father was in his death-bed, with money enough to pay off the mortgage on the farm.

My first experience of the Marks Brothers was in a theatre in London. They were performing Ouida's "Under Two Flags", a thrilling melodrama in which a romantic and beautiful camp follower named Cigarette heroically gave her life to save her lover.

Almost equalling the Marks Brothers in popularity were the Guy Brothers' Minstrels. As well as the standard minstrel show their entertainment included performances by strong men and acrobats. It was the minstrel show, however, that drew the crowds. The black-faced minstrels would sing two or three popular songs, and then the interlocutor would engage in badinage with Rastus, the funny end-man.

Interlocutor:	Rastus, what you doing with that there rope?
Rastus:	This here am a mule rope.
Interlocutor:	What for you got a mule rope?
Rastus:	I'm kind of perplexed about this here mule rope.
Interlocutor:	What am you perplexed about?
Rastus:	I ain't just sure whether I found a rope or lost a mule.

As the twentieth century advanced we saw many memorable productions. It was an age of remarkable creativity. I remember a beautiful production of Maeterlink's "Blue Bird", and a performance of Ibsen's "Doll's House" with Nazimova taking the part of Nora. There were also notable performances of Shakespeare's plays. The Ben Greet Company, for instance, put on delightful productions of his plays out-of-doors. In London they performed on the wooded lawns of Huron College (now expanded into Western University) using almost no props and only such improvised lighting as was readily available.

Pinero and Shaw were the two outstanding dramatists of the period — that is, after Oscar Wilde got into serious trouble for his peccadillos. Pinero was a master of dramatic structure, and skilful at writing sophisticated dialogue. Shaw — well, we didn't know quite how to classify him, but we all went to see his plays. When I was at Queen's University I played a part in Shaw's comedy "You Never Can Tell".

It is notable that the style of acting almost completely changed in the twenty years before the First Great War. The Victorian actor cultivated a beautiful voice with perfect articulation (no gabbling or muttering in the manner of the method actor) and a dignified bearing. I saw Benson play Hamlet in this manner. But this Victorian type of acting was not at all suited to Ibsen or Shaw. The Abbey Theatre in Dublin led the way in introducing a style of acting that was more natural, more spontaneous, and less stilted.

What we old people, however, remember most fondly are the musical comedies of the period. The music was charming, the comedy a riot, and the plot carried you into a never-never land of romantic dreams. The two most famous were "The Merry Widow" and "Floradora" —

"Oh tell me pretty maiden,
Are there any more at home like you? "
Each new operetta – "Babes in Toyland" 1903,
        "Mlle. Modiste" 1905, "The Red Mill" 1906,
            "A Waltz Dream" 1907, and "Naughty Marietta" 1910
                – contained several catchy airs, one of them
always a waltz, which immediately became a hit. Many of the
songs from these comic operas are still being sung, though the
popular singers of today stylize their singing so much that the
charming old tunes are almost unrecognizable.

Sing your senseless modern ditties any way you please,
But don't attempt to mutilate the sweet old melodies;
Oh, I implore the vocalists who bellow, moo, and bawl:
Sing the old songs properly, or sing them not at all.
                – from "Old Songs" by Michael Foran.

It is interesting to note that one of the most popular operettas
before the First Great War, "The Chocolate Soldier" and the
most popular musical after the Second World War, "My Fair
Lady" were both based on plays by George Bernard Shaw.

The first phonographs (usually called talking machines)
appeared not long before the end of the nineteenth century.
Our grocer was the first person in our neighbourhood to get one
of the machines, and one Saturday evening he invited a dozen
youngsters, myself among them, to come and hear it. He and his
family lived behind the store, and very much excited we
assembled in their small parlor.

The talking machine was a strange-looking contraption. It was
operated by a spring motor, which had to be wound up. A wax
record, the shape of a tin can with both ends open, was shoved
on a revolving cylinder. The one thing that at all resembled a
modern hi-fi was the needle, which was placed so that it would
travel in a groove on the wax record. The sound came out
through a large horn. The human voice sounded as if a man as
small as a mouse were speaking into a milk bottle. You had to
listen very carefully to distinguish the words.

The only record I remember was one in which a comic character, called Uncle Josh, told funny stories. And the only story
I remember is one about a bit of trouble Uncle Josh had with
a conductor on a train. After the argument Uncle Josh said:

"But I fooled him. When he finds out, he'll be the maddest conductor on the Pennsylvania Railway. For I bought a round--trip ticket, and I ain't agoin' back."

Caruso, the great Italian tenor, was the first serious artist to record for the phonograph. The extreme resonance of his voice set the needle vibrating with sufficient violence to create a good pattern on the cylinder. Ordinary voices did not record nearly so well. They sounded muted, cracked, and toneless.

Caruso made his first record in 1902. As recording techniques and phonographs both were improved, other artists followed. The Victor Company came out with its famous trade mark, the picture of a fox terrier looking into the horn of a Victor machine, and the caption "His Master's Voice." When the picture was first produced it was a bit optimistic. It would have been a wise dog that knew his own master. All voices sounded more or less alike in the records of the time. But little by little things got better, until the phonograph became, not just a novelty, but a musical instrument of quality.

No one today, when recordings are made by the thousand every year, can understand the excitement with which we looked through each new release of Red Seal records, nor the sacrifices we made to save enough money to buy the record of our choice. The most prized of all these records, the high water--mark of early recording, was the Sextet from "Lucia", in which both Scotti, a famous baritone, and Caruso sang. The quality, the timbre, of the two voices was so much alike, that you could not tell when one singer left off and the other began.

BE IT EVER SO HUMBLE
by John H. Collins

When a person is requested to write an article comparing the average middle-class abode during the years 1895 to 1914, with those in use at the present time, it is a fair assumption on the reader's part that the writer is of such vintage that he has experienced both. In my case, this is true, but I must confess that my memories of the early 1900's are viewed through dimming eyes and vagrant recollections. Also, I feel that the reader must concede that advancing years are prone to stimulate imagination of by-gone days. This, I freely confess, but must insist that the sum and substance of what follows is essentially correct.

It should be understood that my experiences have been restricted to the lower-middle class bracket, with only infrequent glimpses into the homes of the affluent, perhaps as a paper boy or delivery boy. I was, however, much impressed with the glamour of the service quarters. The era of "Victorian" houses ceased in the early 1900s. Skilled craftsmen and an abundance of materials had resulted in many highly decorative homes at that time, most of which have, unfortunately, fallen under the wrecker's hammer.

A comparison of the two periods under consideration is essentially a "physical" one, concerned with the accommodation provided, the various utilities available in each of the periods, and the types of household equipment in use. These various features, however, affected the social life of the occupants and an explanation of these effects must form a part of the comparison.

There were many houses in the early 1900s which depended solely for their winter heat on a pot-bellied wood or coal-burning stove, strategically located and providing a maze of smoke pipe which eventually found its way through as many rooms as possible, thus providing a completely erroneous feeling of warmth.

A humble home

There are many stories recounted, associated with the cleaning of this maze of pipe. Over a period of time the inside became coated with soot or creosote and, in the interests of fire safety, this accumulation must be cleaned out periodically. The pipe was held in place by frequent wire loops and the cleaning process involved a careful step-by-step removal of the hangers, disconnecting of the pipe, cleaning and re-hanging. The trick, of course, was to remove one section without allowing the soot accumulation from all the sections ahead to fall back in a veritable flood-tide, engulfing the cleaner. Even the red flush of anger, rising to the cleaner's face when such a happening occurred, failed to show through the newly acquired ebony hue.

Other than an occasional visit to my grandparents' home, I did not, however, live with such an installation. I do recall, though, the many hours of illicit entertainment provided by the openings in the floors and walls required for the passage of smoke pipe, through which, after being officially relegated to bed, we could listen and sometimes watch the incomprehensible talk and actions of our older relatives.

I do have a vivid recollection of our own homes, modern and up to date at that time, with their coal-fired furnaces in the basement which, assuming proper and adequate attention, provided heating comfort to a reasonable degree in all rooms. "Proper and adequate attention" included the addition of fresh coal at frequent and regular intervals, vigorous shaking of grates to sift out the ash, and finally the disposal of the ash. This ash handling was a household chore frequently delegated (as in my case) to the boys in the family. When the call of street-hockey, skating, or snowball fights was stronger than my sense of duty to household chores, I well remember the philosophical phrase my father used when, upon discovering my dereliction of duty he would resignedly head down the dark cellar stairs muttering —

"Ashes to ashes and dust to dust

If the kids won't sift 'em, the old man must."

Upon completion of my assigned task he would then proceed to one he enjoyed more, using the flat side of a hair brush on the round side of his son.

Humidification in the early heating systems was provided by filling a container on the side of the furnace with water which vaporized with the heat and maintained something we now call "relative humidity" throughout the house. I recall only one occasion when the system caused any problems. One of our coal deliverers, while in the basement, felt a most urgent call of nature, and in desperation used the humidifying tank as a receptacle. It took days to clear the house of the ammonia smell!

Compare the above-described heating procedures with today's gas or oil-fired, push-button controlled, automatic humidification, individual room controls, and total air-conditioning.

There are still many fireplaces as there were in the old days, a carry-over which in most people's opinion is a welcome heritage from the past. What more comforting, relaxing and romantic atmosphere can be produced than that from the warm glow of flickering red, blue and yellow flames, and all the imaginative pictures these conjure up in a mind at ease.

The basements of the late 1800s and early 1900s contained more than a furnace and coal bin. There was inevitably a fruit cellar where home preserves and pickles (now purchased weekly in the supermarket) were stored. A laundry room was essential, equipped with a hand-wringer, galvanized tubs and the old--fashioned corrugated scrub board. The only time I have seen one of these scrub-boards used in the last thirty years was as an instrument in a modern jazz combo. Modern laundries consist of compact, efficient washer and dryer units, and all one requires is a package of detergent and a pile of dirty clothes.

The basement stairs usually led up into the kitchen, a large multipurpose room which served in many cases as kitchen, dining room, family room and general meeting place for family and friends. How often did a harassed mother obtain a momentary respite from her daily chores by sipping a cup of tea with a neighbour whose excuse for coming was to borrow a cup of sugar, but whose reason was to exchange the local gossip.

One of the main differences between the "then" and "now" kitchens, as far as equipment is concerned was the refrigerator. In the "then" days the refrigerator was in reality an ice-box with an upper compartment capable of accommodating up to 50 pounds of block ice. "Behold, the ice man cometh" and a cardboard sign displayed in the front window advised him whether or not ice was needed and, if so, how much.

Another household chore which fell to the lot of the oldest son was to empty the pan under the ice-box before the melted ice overflowed. This abhorrent chore, however, was soon solved by drilling a hole through the floor, hidden from view by the ice-box, thus permitting the melted ice to drip directly onto the earthen floor basement. An old mud hole, under such circumstances, was never of much concern. Our ingenuity at that time did not extend to the point of directing this overflow into the humidifier on the furnace.

Compare the old-time ice-box with our present day, coloured, enamelled, chrome-trimmed, automatic defrosting, ice-cube dispensing kitchen unit, which can hold a full case of beer and still leave plenty of room for food.

The kitchen stove ranged (pardon the pun) from coal or wood fired to gas and in some areas electricity. My personal opinion is that bread and pastries, baked in wood-burning stoves contained something, a hidden taste, aroma or texture which was much superior to those prepared on the new equipment. I am reminded of the cartoon depicting a husband sampling his wife's baking and remarking "I wish you could make bread like mother used to make" to which his wife replied, "I wish you could make dough like father used to make". If compared on the basis of convenience, however, the modern stoves win hands down. The housewife can prepare the food, place it in the oven, set the timer and controls, turn the switch on and go out for the day, fully confident that on her return everything will be cooked to a turn, ready to serve. And if need be, the bread-winner on his return home can remain blissfully ignorant of his wife's absence.

The size of the old-fashioned kitchens was often sufficiently large to serve as a playroom for the children, directly under the supervision of the harassed mother as she cooked, washed or gossipped. Modern homes often provide a playroom or play area directly visible from the compact, unitized kitchen where the mother can perform her miracles, unimpeded by roller skates, tricycles, doll carriages or hockey sticks.

The remainder of the ground floor consisted usually of a separate dining room for state occasions, a living room and in many cases a parlour. This latter room was restricted to whatever formal entertaining might be done, such as a visit from the local minister, the women's sewing circle, serious talks regarding one's intentions as far as the daughter was concerned, and for "wakes" which were a normal part of any bereavement ceremonies.

Bathroom facilities in modern homes are much more generous than at the turn of the century. Nowadays it is the rule rather than the exception to have a "His" and "Hers" complete with all the essential fixtures. In earlier days one bathroom served the entire family regardless of its size, and it was often necessary to introduce a ticket system, when each took his number and awaited his turn. The larger the family the more frequent the mishaps! The bathroom fixtures have come a long way in terms of design and function. Tubs were formerly free--standing, on ornate feet and the throne was a wooden-seated, pull-chain affair, as compared to our modern built-in tubs and

and silent, push-button W.C.'s — all in colour to suit the Owner's fancy. And compare the old-fashioned pig tail light bulb with the modern fluorescent, concealed fixtures which provide adequate light to all parts of the bathroom. This has eliminated the sight of a businessman appearing for work with one side of his face clean-shaven and the other covered with stubble. The physical size of these rooms has also undergone a marked change. Modern ablution facilities are compact, permitting of only single occupancy, while the old ones were spacious enough to allow for morning calisthenics, including push-ups, without danger of becoming entangled in one way or another with the plumbing fixtures.

The change in the exterior appearance of houses of the early 1900's and those of today is startling. Where are the old-fashioned verandahs from which the occupants could supervise all their neighbours' activities, gossip across the railings or brace one's feet against the rail and do nothing? Present day outdoor living is done on a completely private patio (often complete with swimming pool), screened from the neighbours by a hedge or ornate fence. The result of this arrangement is, of course, to prevent any neighbourly back-fence gossip, necessitating some more devious means of learning one's neighbour's private affairs.

Housewives of today do not even have the opportunity of backyard gossip when they are hanging out clothes. The modern washers and dryers have completely eliminated the homey sight of a clothesline with its longjohns happily waving arms and legs at all who cared to look. And in the wintertime those same arms and legs, frozen stiff, would swing their paralyzed selves in a rhythmic pendulum-fashion and when the washing was taken in it was a simple matter to merely stand them in a corner.

And while we are in the backyard, let's talk about the vegetable gardens. Most people cultivated a small patch to provide peas, carrots and beets for their table, onions for their martinis and a sprig of mint for their gin. Nowadays, one might find a well-concealed box or pot of cannibis, a well-known anodyne and sedative, used chiefly for coughs and bronchitis.

One of the most obvious changes in the exterior appearance of houses is the myriad of porcupine quills piercing the.

atmosphere to catch the sight and sound of such things as the Watergate soap opera, Marcus Welby, M.D. and various sports events.

There are many other changes in the development of domestic architecture, between what might be called the Victorian Era and our present modern or contemporary style; for example, the use of leaded glass in windows and doors, combination storm and screen windows which remain in place throughout the entire year, and the use of ornamentation or gables, cornices, dormers, etc., which are frequently referred to as "ginger bread". One of the redeeming features of "ginger bread" was the knowledge that a great part of it was hand-crafted, and bespoke highly of the skills of the tradesmen. So many of our building components today are prefabricated or machine made that the "pride of accomplishment" of former days is missing. Granted, the "ginger bread" added nothing to the comfort or efficiency of the home, and in some instances the design struck a discordant note, nevertheless those houses had an individual charm which is often now missing from our mass-produced, stereotyped middle class housing developments.

As a former occupant of the "Victorian" type house, I fear that any comparisons I might make are tinged with a strong element of nostalgia. Despite this fact, I have succumbed to the modern trend and now live in one of our thousands of high-rise, comfortable apartment buildings (sometimes referred to as "concrete filing cabinets"). As I approach senility, I find the conveniences of this type of living a welcome substitute for the grass-cutting, snow-shovelling, garden-weeding life of earlier days when such activities were an outlet for exuberant youth as compared to today's arthritic lassitude. Despite this change in attitude, I still spend many hours reminiscing about life in the good old days.

NEWSPAPERS

by Dora Macdonald

Newspapers in the years just before and just after the turn of the century were different from newspapers today in one important regard. In those days the tenor of life was so even and so pleasant that at least locally newsworthy events rarely occurred. When normal people are living normal more or less happy lives, what is there to report? A run-away horse perhaps; a speech by some local politician (just as dull then as now); a visit from the bishop; very rarely a good, juicy murder. But day after day nothing at all.

One editor of a small town newspaper expressed his feelings as follows:

"News, news, news! It's enough to give a man the blues,
Nobody married, and nobody dead; nobody broken an arm
or a head;
No one got run in for taking a horn; nobody buried and nobody born;
Oh, for a racket, a riot, a fuss! Someone to come in and kick
up a muss.
Somebody thumped within an inch of his life; somebody run
off with another man's wife;
Someone come in and paid up his dues; anything, anything,
just so it's news."

As society reporter on a small town newspaper during the early years of the century, I know exactly how that editor felt. Day after day I would spend hours on the telephone trying to get something to fill my column — a euchre party, a visitor from out-of-town, an engagement to be announced, even a birthday in the family. Believe me, when I got even a snippet of real news, I made the most of it. It was a frustrating business.

In lieu of hard news stories, the newspapers of the period published literary articles and poems. Typical of the interests of the time was an account in one paper of Thomas Carlyle's life and work. Does anybody today ever read that morose writer's solemn sermonizing? I doubt it. Today the nearest any newspaper ever comes to a literary essay is an extended book review, a snappy article about some television personality who has already received more publicity than his limited talents deserve, or an article about some sports celebrity.

Some of the poetry that appeared in the dailies in the old days was pretty awful stuff. I remember that we used to receive in the mail some of the worst doggerel I ever read written by a woman who signed herself G. Pearl Potter, Poetess. Would that I had saved some of her effusions! Her lyrical outbursts were finally quenched when the proprietor of the paper in desperation set a charge of 30 cents a line for the publication of poetry. But much of the poetry was passable. Not up to the standard of Tennyson, or even Browning. But not bad. Some of the poems were not only read but cherished.

In my possession is a scrapbook of newspaper clippings, which was started by some unknown person in the nineties of last century and continued well into this century. In this scrapbook are scores of poems clipped from the daily newspapers. Many of the poems point a moral. The poets of the period were much given to singing the joys of the simple life — the joy of sitting by your own fireside (in those days we weren't dependent on Arab sheiks for our home comfort) with your babe on your knee, and your wife knitting on the other side of the fireplace. Or they deplored man's foolishness in not valuing the good things of life until they were lost — not valuing good clear water until the well went dry, or the love of a friend until that friend is dead.

Contentment with one's lot was lauded as a cardinal virtue.

BE   CONTENT

If others are wealthy while we are but poor,
  We still may be happy as they,
For moderate desire, not immoderate store,
  Best keeps discontentment away.

The noblest and richest have troubles to bear,
  Amid their possessions untold,
Of suffering and sorrow they all have their share,
  In spite of their riches and gold.

If duty be done 'tis a far greater thing,
  Than riches or honor or gain;
With this even a cottage will happiness bring,
  Without it a palace were vain.

The philosophy of that poem is rather different from the philosophy that is dinned into our ears every day and all day, the philosophy of our buy-now-pay-later civilization, a philosophy of divine discontent with our limited means. We are urged "for any good reason" to borrow up to $10,000 from one or other finance company. Newspaper advertisements invite us to purchase this or that unnecessary article with no down payment, just so much a month. (For how long we are, of course, not told.) Credit cards have supplanted money in the daily exchange. If we open our wallets and offer to pay cash for what we purchase in any place but the supermarket, we are looked on as being a bit queer.

* * *

The newspaper of the period usually contained at least one humorous item, often an anecdote about an Irishman. For some reason Irishmen were always supposed to be making bulls.

In my time I have known many Irish men and Irish women but I have never known one who was any more given than the rest of us to committing ludicrous inconsistencies of speech. But here is what was described as a "rale Irish letter" in an old newspaper:

"Dear nefue,—

I haen't sint yes a letther since the last time I wrote to yes because we've moved from the former place of livin, and I didn't know whether the letther wud reach yes or not. I now wid pleasure take my pen in hand to inform yes of the death of yer own livin uncle Kilpatrick, who died suddenly after a lingering illness of six months. I am at a loss to tell what caused his death, but I fear it was his last illness. He niver was well ten days together durin the hull time of his confinement. But I fear he died of atin too much paze and gravy. Be that as it will, he had no sooner breathed his last, than the doctor gave up all hope of his recovery.

Hopin you are doin well in America, I remain

Your lovin' grandfather,
Mike Maguire."

Sure and if there is an Irishman alive who speaks like that, he's been dead these seventy years, for I never heard the likes of that talk from anyone.

* * *

The woman's section of the paper, of course, contained recipes. Often these recipes gave advice to the housewife on such matters as preserving fruit or making pickles. Often they advised her how to save a penny.

"A very convenient mucilage can be made out of onion juice. A good-sized Spanish onion, after being boiled a short time, will yield on being pressed quite a large quantity of very adhesive fluid. This fluid is just as good for most purposes as any costly mucilage."

How would you like to get a letter from your love tightly sealed and sweetly scented with the juice of an onion? In the topsy-turvy world we live in today, the onion would, of course, be far more costly than the mucilage.

At the turn of the century Friday was bargain day at all the big stores. And of course the newspapers profited by the advertising. In Toronto the two big department stores, Eaton's and Simpson's, would each take sometimes as much as two whole columns on Thursday to advertise their Friday bargains. To make modern bargain hunters green with envy, I'll quote some prices from a Simpson advertisement which appeared in the Mail and Empire in the mid-nineties.

Ladies' Hand-trimmed Oxford Shoes	$ .69
Ladies' Drawers (now called panties)	$ .17
Pair of Blankets	$ 1.50
Men's Shirts	$ .50
Solid Oak Bedroom Suite, Cheval Mirror	$19.25
Black Silk Taffeta, rustling kind (per yard)	$ .50

Imagine walking up a ball-room floor in a black taffeta dress which rustled. What a sensation you would make!

To show that even in those days Eaton's would not be undersold, let me quote from one of their advertisements of about the same date.

White Cotton Gowns, 2 rows cluster tucks, 2 rows insertion, cambric frill around neck and down front	$ .47

This of course would be a nightgown, and not one of those waltz-length affairs, but full length, dropping not only below the knees but below the ankles. And with all those tucks and frills and insertions — wow!

White Cotton Skirts	$ .35
Men's fine wool socks (a pair)	$ .20
Chocolate (a pound)	$ .10
Ladies' White Cotton Drawers, tucks and cambric frill	$ .20

Admittedly these drawers (panties) were 3c more than Simpson's, but they had tucks and frills. And what girl would not gladly pay 3c extra for tucks and frills on her drawers?

Apparently they had dedicated men in white coats carrying out research for their commercials even in the nineties. The following advertisement appeared in a newspaper of the period:

"Eight samples of the principal Canadian, American and English salts convinced one of the best chemists in the country that Windsor Salt contained practically 30 per cent less impurity than any of the other seven samples. Ask your grocer for Windsor Table Salt."

* * *

Some of the advertising, it must be admitted, revealed the seamier side of Victorian and Edwardian life. From a single issue of the St. Thomas "Daily Times", I offer the following advertisements in somewhat abbreviated form:

CURE YOURSELF

Use BIG G for Gonorrhea, Gleet, Supermatorrhea, Whites, unnatural discharges. Cures in 1 to 5 days Guarranteed.
And again:

INDAPO

The Great Hindoo Remedy
Cures all Nervous Diseases, Failing Memory,
Paresis, Sleeplessness, Nightly Emissions caused
by past abuses, gives vigor and size to shrunken organs.

Price $1.00 a bottle.

Accompanying the latter advertisement were four progressive pictures of a sufferer who was cured. In the first picture (labelled 1st day) you see a broken-down wretch, hollow-cheeked, baggy-eyed, with drooping shoulders and sadly drooping moustache. In the second (10th day) his chest is filling out, his cheeks are not so sunken, his shoulders don't droop so badly, and (mark this) his moustache is beginning to show some life. In the third (20th day) the man looks quite normal. Even his moustache has ceased to droop. The last picture (30th) day shows a barrel-chested strong man, with square shoulders and fully rounded cheeks. And (mark this well) the moustache has not only ceased to droop. It is curled up in the perkiest manner.

What a marvelous concoction Indapo must have been!

Edward Bok, the editor of "The Ladies' Home Journal", for years carried on a vigorous campaign against such fraudulent advertising, a campaign which was ultimately successful. He directed his attention, not only to the advertising of supposed cures for V.D., but also against Lydia Pinkham, who was giving advice to suffering women long after she was dead and buried, advice which always included the taking of Lydia Pinkham's Vegetable Compound for female disorders.

* * *

Sixty years ago there were many more newspapers than there are today. Almost every town had at least two, one liberal and one conservative. Believe me, people took their politics seriously in those days. The two most popular Toronto morning papers had a wide circulation throughout the province. But good Liberals would rather be found dead than be seen reading the "Mail and Empire". And good Conservatives accepted as gospel truth every word in the "Mail and Empire" and snorted at the holy "Globe" with its sanctimonious editorials.

The Woodstock "Sentinel-Review" was a liberal newspaper. At one time Andrew Patullo, who was a staunch Liberal and for many years a member of the provincial Legislature, was proprietor, but when I was associated with the paper, it had passed into the hands of an energetic dapper little man called Billy Taylor. Taylor was a bachelor, who devoted all his affection and all his energies to the newspaper. At the time there were three newspapers in Woodstock, a town of less than ten thousand inhabitants, the "Sentinel-Review", the "Express", and the "Times". Ultimately the enterprising "Sentinel-Review" crowded out the other two.

By 1914 the modern newspaper was well on its way. It not only told its readers what was going in in the world, but it purveyed entertainment, and kept them up to date in a wide variety of fields. Any newspaper of any account had its sports section, its women's section (even more gushing than such sections are today) and its comic section, with Jiggs and Maggie, Mutt and Jeff, and Buster Brown. The columnist with a by-line was there also, sometimes chatting about everyday affairs with whimsical humor, like Peter McArthur, sometimes expressing highly personal views more seriously, like McAree. The more pretentious dailies usually produce special editions once a week, perhaps an edition with a section of special interest to rural communities, and on Saturday perhaps an edition with more general articles for Sunday reading. On Thursdays the "Sentinel-Review", a very progressive paper, published two distinct editions, one city, the other rural. The rural edition was in reality a weekly newspaper for farmers. It had a wide circulation throughout Oxford county.

MEMORIES OF A NEWSPAPER WOMAN

by Dora Macdonald

When I graduated from high school I first got a job in the office of a soap factory, but before two years were up I heard of a vacancy with the "Sentinel-Review" that was better paid and more to my liking. I made application, was interviewed by Mr. Taylor, the proprietor, and was taken on at once. He assigned me to the circulation department in the general office. But before very long I was given a more responsible job, probably because I had a fair command of the English language. My father was a stickler for good English. He insisted on our speaking correctly, and encouraged us to develop an extensive vocabulary.

I was made assistant to the Editor of "Rod and Gun", at that time a very successful magazine for sportsmen. The Editor was an ugly but engaging little Englishman with a brain, named Arthur Harvey Smith. From him I learned how a popular magazine should be edited.

But he had one defect. He spoke with a stammer. He would balk over a word, you would try to help him, but it was useless. He would always go back and repeat what he had been trying to say.

His wife wore the most outrageous hats I ever saw, outrageous even for those days. They were piled high with ribbons and flowers.

From there I went to the editorial office of the newspaper, where I carried on such a variety of jobs that I got a real insight into the workings of an enterprising small-town newspaper. In that office I edited the country news, went over the exchange newspapers, making clippings of anything that might be of interest to any of the editors, pinch-hit for the proof-reader when she left, until I kicked at the extra work and a new proof-reader was appointed, and ultimately became Society Editor. Taylor seemed to think that I could do almost anything.

An outrageous hat

At one time he said, "Damn it, Miss Dugit, if you weren't a girl, I would make you city editor. At least you wouldn't get drunk."

At that time it was pretty well taken for granted that all newspaper men were heavy drinkers. Taylor himself was no saint, but he never let alcohol interfere with his work.

In addition to all the other jobs, I was secretary to John Markey, the general editor, who wrote all the newspaper's editorials.

John Markey was a remarkable man. He said that he came to this country "a barefoot Irish spalpeen with little schooling and no money." But he worked up to be one of the best educated men I ever knew. Music, art, poetry, literature of all sorts — he knew them all, and more besides. He was a very able dramatic critic. Once I went to a play in which May Robson starred. Next morning I burbled with enthusiasm for May's marvellous gift for comedy.

"Miss Dugit", he said," when an actress gives a revolting imitation of vomitting on the stage, that is farce, not comedy."

And then he went on to explain the difference. "Farce may be good for a laugh, sometimes a hilarious laugh. Farce presents a situation where something is badly out of kilter, ludicrous because it is completely unexpected. We may laugh at a pompous alderman who slips on a banana peel and falls on his rump; we laugh at the startling transformation of stiff dignity into sprawling helplessness. Last night we laughed uproariously because we were shocked by the sudden intrusion of nauseating vulgarity into a scene that was otherwise highly decorous. But real comedy, true humor has more to it than that. True comedy displays a depth of human understanding, sometimes even a touch of pathos, completely lacking in farce."

He was one of those Irishmen who have a natural affinity for books, and a keen sensitivity to literary and artistic values. I owe a great deal to Mr. Markey. To be sure I was always attracted by good books. I was reading Dickens when I was five years old, that is before I ever went to school. But Mr. Markey was largely responsible for forming and directing my interest in things of the mind. At Christmas he always gave me a present of a good book.

And he said, "Miss Dugit..."

But perhaps I should explain here that first names were not commonly used sixty years ago. The practice of calling people by their Christian names came in with the spread of the Rotary and Kiwanis clubs. At that time I was plump and as a rule amiable. Around the office I was known as Cherub. But Mr. Markey always used my surname.

"Miss Dugit, always read everything that is available, and you will never be at a loss for something to do. And gradually you

The editor

will come to differentiate between what is good, and what is not so good."

He had an excellent gramaphone, excellent, that is, for those days. Miss Moysey, an older woman on the staff, and I spent many evenings at his home just listening to records. I can still see him with his eyes closed blissfully drinking in the music. He was particularly addicted to Russian music, which at that time consisted almost altogether of Tchaikovsky.

How John Markey and Taylor ever got along together is a mystery. No two men could be more different. Billy Taylor was an energetic businessman, a real entrepreneur, with no interest whatever in cultural matters. He was a neat dapper little man, very fussy about his personal appearance. He was reputed to have thirty suits in his wardrobe.

John Markey, on the other hand, looked as if he were made of spare parts that didn't quite fit together. Tall, shambling, loose-jointed, he rambled along the sidewalk oblivious to what was happening 'round about him. His clothes were never properly pressed, and he always wore a battered old broad-brimmed fedora, very shabby. From time to time his wife would hide the old hat (she didn't dare throw it away) and buy him a new one. For a few days, very ill at ease, he would wear the new hat. But somehow or other he would always dig up the old one, and perfectly happy, would resume wearing it.

Taylor took great pride in his paper. He was shrewd enough to know that the respect with which the paper was regarded among thoughtful people was largely the result of Markey's cogent and thoughtful editorials. He himself took great pains to see that everything was as it should be in each new issue. He would grab the first copy off the press each day, sit down in the office and go through it carefully. If he came on a bloomer, he would give vent to an explosive "Damn" (a very bad word in those days), leap to his feet like a jack-rabbit, bound up the stairs two steps at a time, and woe to the head of the composing room, John McLean!

In his own way John McLean was as able as any man on the staff. He was responsible for the make-up of the paper, and he took great pride in making it look smart and attractive. Though he was a Scot, he always declared that he knew no Gaelic. But on Hogmanay (New Year's Eve) he would always become gloriously drunk, and would stagger home at two or three in the morning roaring Gaelic songs at the top of his lungs.

One of Taylor's special gifts was the ability to collect around him men of talent. He had a genius for recognizing real worth. John Stronach was for a time city editor. He was another Scot, a graduate of Edinborough University, and he had a real flair for journalism. He was followed by Charlie Hamblyn. Charlie was the handsome guy of the crowd, a real Adonis with classical features and ambrosial curls like Tennyson's Aphrodite. It was said that at one time or another he made love to every girl in Woodstock, without becoming serious about any one. Every girl, that is, except me. My brothers said I was too damned independent. Charlie preferred the clinging-vine type.

It was characteristic of the time that the girls on the staff seemed to be pretty much run-of-the-mill. In those days women were not expected to distinguish themselves. But there was one exception. Blanche Hume looked like a little old maid, but she possessed devastating wit and boundless energy. She would stop at nothing. On one occasion she went to Alberta as a reporter with a mountain climbing party. Everybody expected that she would stay at the foot of the mountain. But no chance. She proved to be one of the best climbers of the lot. When Arthur Harvey Smith retired she became Editor of "Rod and Gun". But ultimately she left the "Sentinel-Review" to serve as Lorne Pierce's assistant at the Ryerson Press. If Blanche had lived in a later generation, when more important positions were opening up for women, there is no telling what she might have achieved.

As I sit here peacefully knitting, and looking back over the years, one scene after another flits before my mind I remember vividly the turmoil in the office between three and four every afternoon. Everybody was rushing about and falling over each other to get ready a bundle of papers for the inter-city trolley which passed the office at four o'clock sharp. We had a large circulation in Ingersoll, a neighboring town. I can remember vividly how we received our national and foreign news. It was tapped out on an old-fashioned telegraph instrument in the telegraph office down the street. And the manager who was lame would bring the message to us himself. I can still hear him stamping up the iron stairs one step at a time and cursing all news-hungry editors as he went. I recall my experiences as a strike-breaker. The men in the press room went out on strike, demanding a closed shop, something that was very unpopular with management in those days. Taylor got me to operate one of the old monoline machines. Ordinarily we used the much more modern linotype machines, but they could not be operated by a mere typist. The tips of my fingers are still somewhat insensitive to heat, because when I made a mistake I would impatiently grab the hot metal without waiting for it to cool.

There was one occasion when I disgraced myself. One Sunday Bishop Farthing of Montreal preached in our church, and I reported his sermon for the paper. It must have been a good report, for several members of the congregation complimented me, and the Bishop himself thanked me. So much praise must have gone to my head. Later in the week Newton Wesley Rowell visited our town. He was touring the province speaking on his favorite topic, "Banish the bar, and save the boys". I undertook to take down his speech in shorthand. But he rattled away with the speed of a machine-gun. In five minutes I was so confused that I completely lost track of what he was saying. My report was a mess.

As editor of the rural news I remember receiving the usual would-be cute remarks. "Joe Smith is smiling today. It's a boy." Or, "Ed Smilie has been seen driving up John Turner's lane several evenings this week. I wonder why! " Sometimes, however, I had to suppress unprintable crudities. "The undertaker has been doing a roaring business this week, with two dead and another on the way."

My most amusing experiences were probably as Society Editor. One woman in a near-by village was an indefatigable news collector. She used to call me at all hours on the telephone. If I am not mistaken we used to pay her so much a line for what we printed. Once she told me about a girl in the village who was to be married. When I asked her for details of the wedding, she said: "You just stay on the line, Miss Dudge-et, and I'll call her mother." The girl's mother babbled

143

away for half-an-hour about the wedding, quite unaware that a newspaper reporter was making notes of everything she said.

One other experience I'll never forget was the Rolph wedding. Mrs. Rolph took in washing and went out by the day as a cleaning woman. She was full of energy. But she was one of the ugliest women I ever knew. She always wore a tattered old coat which her husband had discarded, and a peaked cap which had also been his. Her husband (she called him old Rolph) did odd jobs around town. His idea of working was to earn enough money to buy a bottle of whisky, and then to go on a binge. Well, Helen, one of Mrs. Rolph's daughters (she had ten children) was about to be married. Helen was not a bad looking girl in a sonsy way.

A few days before the wedding Mrs. Rolph barged into the office looking for me.

"Miss Dudge-et," she said, "it's you who writes these society notes, isn'it?"

"Yes."

"Our Helen — I always calls her Hellie for short — well, dear little Hellie is being married."

"So I hear."

"Now, Miss Dudge-et, couldn't you write up a real nice account of dear little Hellie's wedding?"

"We don't always..."

"Just this once, Miss Dudge-et. We want to send it back to England, so that our folks there will see that we really count for something out here."

"Whom is she going to marry?"

"Tom McGuire. You know, he's stable boy over at the livery stable. But you don't need to mention that. Couldn't you just call him a prominent citizen of Woodstock?

By this time I was entering into the spirit of the occasion.

After some thought, I said, "Would it do if I called him Thomas II. McGuire, well known for his interest in spirited horses?"

"That will knock Uncle Billy silly, the old goat. He always said me and old Rolph wouldn't amount to anything."

"What is the bride going to wear?"

"A white silk gown with plenty of tucks and frills, and a veil.

A. M.

Thomas H. McGuire

It was wore by two other brides before it come to dear little Hellie. And it's too long for her. But I'm going to pin it up in front so as it will have a train."

"What is the groom going to give the bride for a wedding present?"

This stumped Mrs. Rolph.

"I never thought of that," she said, "but you just wait and I'll call you back."

Whenever I asked for a further detail, I sent Mrs. Rolph into a tizzy. But she always came up with an answer. When I finished, I had produced an account of the wedding that would be a huge laugh to those who knew the people concerned, but would sound very impressive to the relatives back in England.

It was in my most impressionable years, from the late teens on into the twenties that I worked on a newspaper. I worked hard, but I enjoyed every minute of it. There was a spirit of camaraderie in the office. We worked as a team, and were proud of what we produced. Now that I am no longer young, now that I am full of years and a bit arthritic, it is to that period that my mind naturally goes back. I suppose all old people are like that. When our minds are empty of daily cares, when dusk is falling on our days, we often sit and dream. And it is then that scenes from that age of long ago —

> "Flash upon that inward eye,
> Which is the bliss of solitude."

MANNERS AND MORALS OF TWO DECADES
by Viola Whitney Pratt

"It was the best of times, it was the worst of times, it was the age of wisdom, it was the age of foolishness, it was the epoch of belief, it was the epoch of incredulity, it was the season of light, it was the season of darkness, it was the spring of hope, it was the winter of despair, we had everything before us, we had nothing before us, we were all going direct to Heaven, we were all going direct the other way — in short, the period was so far like the present period, that some of its noisiest authorities insisted on its being received, for good or for evil, in the superlative degree of comparison only."

This did Dickens depict the years which ushered in the 18th century; his words are just as suitable for the end of that century and for the beginning of our own. The last ten years of the 19th century have been called "the naughty nineties" or more optimistically "the portals to the age of gold". It is indeed true that manners and morals, tossed about in the maelstrom of man's history and vicissitudes, can never emerge as black or white, no matter what our nostalgic memories may claim for them.

Our society is chained to slogans. Each generation comes limping along with shibboleths tied to its ankles or else borne aloft like banners in the sunlit sky. The language of today is riddled with them: "Do your own thing";"Don't lose your cool"; "Make love, not war"; "Why wait for spring, do it now? "; "Feed your head" (not with books, but drugs) — the list grows continually, but in the first years of this century there was a long list too: "Spare the rod and spoil the child"; "Children should be seen and not heard"; "It is a sin to steal a pin"; "There's not to question why"; "Be good, sweet maid, and let who will be clever". These were standard precepts on which to build the manners and morals of the day. And so, on the surface, life in village, town and city went on its harmonious way, like the measures of a well-ordered minuet.

For manners really were taught in those days. On the top shelf of the bookcase in our parlour, along with the Bible, Pilgrim's Progress, Johnson's Lives of the Poets, the Collected Works of Tennyson and Browning, there reposed, quite unashamedly, at home, a beautifully bound book on Etiquette. It contained everything a well-bred man or woman should know about manners and morals — how to write a letter for every occasion, the correct procedure for a marriage proposal, when to make a formal or informal call, the use of fish knives and forks — a complete guide to the complicated pattern of living. No child came to the table unwashed or uncombed, nor did he speak out of turn. He was taught never to sit while an older person stood, to remove his hat on stated occasions, and when in doubt to follow the golden rule.

Morals were taught too, and in abundance. Every child of my acquaintance knew the Ten Commandments by heart; every book we read (except those hidden beneath the mattress) was full of moral precepts. "Eric" or "Little by Little", the Elsie books, and "The Lamplighter", for instance, contained enough ethical proddings to last for a lifetime of rectitude; the poems of Jane Taylor indicated quite closely the path good children should take, and the punishments meted out to those who strayed from the narrow road of virtue. The stories in our school books usually contained a hidden or an obvious moral. In "Casabianca", the boy who stood on the burning deck was the epitome of obedience; "the little girl who was always going to" was duly punished; the would-be May Queen was so pricked by conscience over a deception that she refused the May Day crown, and rushed home crying "No Crown for me! No Crown for me! " The fillers at the bottom of the pages were made up of such edifying reminders as:

> "If little labour, little are our gains,
> Man's fortunes are according to his pains."

> "Howe'er it be, it seems to me
> 'Tis only noble to be good."

> "Let your truth stand sure, and the world is true;
> Let your heart keep pure, and the world will too."

At the turn of the century many pleasures were sinful: dancing, card playing, theatre-going. I remember as a child seeing a jack of spades lying face up on the sidewalk, and crossing to the other side of the street, lest I be contaminated by too close an exposure to this instrument of the devil. When I was about eleven, I somehow obtained a ticket for a performance in the town theatre, and begged my parents to allow me to go. "I should think it would be all right," said my kind and tolerant father, "since it is called 'The Prodigal Son' ". Though the very naughty, and, I expect, pornographic story had little in common with the Biblical one, I sat entranced in the front seat, enjoying a vicarious and wholly delightful wickedness. I was only allowed to go to a movie (in its earliest days) because the daughter of a highly respectable judge was taking me. I remember little about it except that a very large pair of corsets in a lady's bedroom was thrown through the air, the only elevated thing in a peculiarly drab performance. As late as 1912, the Dean of the College I attended said to me with a sigh as I was leaving for the Royal Alex to see a performance of Macbeth: "Now is the time I regret that my principles will not allow me to go to the theatre."

But morals could sink just as low in 1900 as in any decade before or after. It was whispered among the gossips that our village beauty was not all she should be, and that a jaunty new arrival had once served a prison sentence. My Sunday School teacher eloped with her father's hired man, and never went to church again. The year Queen Victoria died there were three murders in our village and they made scarcely a ripple in its moral pond. Two of the murderers remained respectable citizens; the third murderer disappeared for good on the morning of this crime, but it was a most thrilling day for us, because this murder was committed on our property, and my father discovered the victim — a remittance man from Scotland, we later discovered.

When I was an undergraduate in residence, we had many distinguished women as house guests – some of whom were trying desperately to change the mores and social temper of the day. Emmeline Pankhurst visited us briefly in the heyday of her notoriety, when St. Paul's idea of submissive, be-hatted women was still firmly held by the majority of people. But the two iconoclasts I remember most vividly were Dr. Marie Stopes and a Russian princess whose name I never did pronounce. She was an ardent suffragette and had been imprisoned two or three times for her revolutionary ideas. She was beautiful as the dawn, and like the dawn, glowing and unpredictable. Every evening of her stay, we sat at her feet and learned from her how manners and morals must never be static nor stereotyped, and that we who were young and intelligent should help to change them.

But the woman who did more than any other to pioneer new codes of morality and shatter the old ones, was Dr. Marie Stopes, who spent almost a week in full residence. Since it happened to be my turn to sit at the head table, I was expected to entertain her. But it was she who entertained me; she was a most brilliant woman with doctorates in Science and Philosophy, a noted paleontologist and an individual who did her own thing with a vengeance. She came down to dinner every night dressed more like the Begum of Dudha than a college professor (at the age of 25 she became the first woman professor of science at Manchester University), and she talked gaily on many erudite subjects – fossils, coal, research, bio-chemistry, the drama in Japan, the perils of the Black Forest, the varieties of men in her life. On her last evening with us she told us she was getting married the next day. The week before she came to us she had met a young Canadian doctor of Science at a conference in St. Louis and had become engaged to him almost at once. The marriage was not a success, but it led to the writing of her book, Married Love, which in 1918 sold over a million copies, and started her on a new career which for a time made her the most famous and infamous woman of her day as the pioneer advocate of sexual freedoms, family planning and birth control.

Another woman who did not visit us, but whom we knew as the best-known American woman of that decade, and whose fictional autobiography was a best-seller in 1910, was Jane Addams. I was told a story about her by one of the young women who worked with her in Hull House in the 1890s — — story which illustrates my contention that manners and morals are built on very shifting sands indeed.

Jane Addams was founder of Hull House in Chicago, the first and best-known settlement of its kind in America, and she was hostess to a stream of guests from around the world. Two women high in British society at one point posed a problem. They both smoked cigarettes! Now in the America of the 1890s no women would be seen smoking except prostitutes, a poetess or two, and a few other presumably lost souls. To Jane Addams, however, the question was one, not of morals, but of manners. She called her staff of women together and explained the situation. "I want our distinguished guests to feel at home," she said, "and to smoke without embarrassment. Therefore, I should like two of you to volunteer to smoke while our guests are there whenever the occasion requires." Two young women volunteered, and the visit was a tremendous success.

If these reflections on some social aspects of the early 20th century in Ontario seem slanted towards the distaff side, I will take refuge in another popular quotation of that day. "The hand that rocks the cradle is the hand that rules the world." There were a great many energetic cradle-rockers in those days bent on revolutionizing both the cradles and their occupants. But after 1914 it was neither suffragettes nor other reformers, but unforeseen forces let loose by war which were to rock our world to its foundations, and rearrange or destroy most of the patterns which had shaped our manners and controlled our moral codes.

QUEER MORAL STANDARDS

by Norman McPherson

When several of us read Dr. Viola Pratt's article we were startled to learn that in our youth many people considered us to be headed straight for hell. She writes: "At the turn of the century many pleasures were sinful: dancing, card playing, theatre-going." Many of us took to these pleasures as fish take to water. Helen Ball can't remember when she first learned to play cards, though she admits that she did not go to dances until she was eighteen. Others of us were organizing dances when we were in high school. Dora Macdonald learned to count by playing cribbage and she was playing whist and euchre with older people when she was ten. Adrian Macdonald became expert at bridge by playing with theology students when he was at college. And the only thing that prevented us from going to the theatre often was lack of cash. The truth is that Viola was brought up in a strict Methodist home, while many of us came from Anglican, Presbyterian, or Catholic homes.

As we look back over the years we realize that many of the ethical taboos that prevailed when we were young were queer, incomprehensible to young people today. Each religious denomination cherished its own pet taboos, and looked down on all the others as somewhat remiss, sometimes with scorn. When church union was being considered, a scotch Presbyterian minister said, "I canna gae with those ungodly Methodists, or those slipshod Congregationalists; I'd rather gie up religion a-together and gae with the Anglicans." Our attitude towards sex, though it was an extreme form of an age-old tradition, is puzzling, almost laughable to people today. The change in attitude was brought about by Havelock Ellis and Freud, especially Freud. When I was at college a professor in the philosophy department said that Freud caused as great a revolution in our thinking as had Darwin. Then even more than now the attitudes towards alcohol differed widely. Anglicans and Catholics favored moderation. But among Methodists,

Baptists, and Presbyterians there were many fanatical prohibitionists. The Women's Christian Temperance Union really got going in the early years of the century. One old minister (I refrain from saying to which denomination he belonged) was not averse to having an occasional snort; but, for fear of the teetotal members of his congregation, he was forced to bring his whisky home in a coal oil can One of the strongest tendencies of the period was to ban certain words as wicked. Michael Foran, a member of our group, has been mentioned elsewhere as a poet worthy of note. He wrote his first poem when he was in Wingham High School. On one occasion the school put on a St. Patrick's Day concert A choir of girls all dressed in green sang a comic song about a storekeeper who put up a sign with the name Kelly spelled with one "L". The concluding two lines of the song were —

> "If I knock the 'L' out of Kelly
> He'll knock the 'L' out of me."

This harmless witticism caused an uproar among the teachers on the staff. They were shocked, scandalized, horrified that nice girls should even hint at such a wicked word as "hell". Next day one straight-laced old biddie burst into tears when she reproached her class for this appalling breach of propriety.

Every fortnight the school issued what was described as a magazine, though it was in reality little more than a pamphlet. Michael was editor.

In the issue following this episode he wrote —

> "The Wingham girls are the funniest girls
>   That I have ever seen;
> I wouldn't dare let them hear me swear,
>   They'd sock me on the bean.
> But they sang a bit at the high school Lit,
>   And every fair collen —
> If they didn't say 'hell', they might just as well,
>   For we all know what they mean."

COUSIN BERTHA

by Helen Ball

She was a big woman and she wore the long caped coat of an Anglican Deaconess with an air of severe authority. A Queen Victoria bonnet tied under her chin with broad ribbons completed the costume. It was oddly becoming to a face spoken of by her associates as sadly sweet. True, her eyes were pale and gentle but the sanctimonious set of her mouth and the inquisitive length of her nose belied, for me, any claim to sweetness.

Her life was given to good works. Day after day she attended Magistrate's Court ready to take under her ample wing any wayward girls remanded into her custody. Her job in a joyless and wicked world was to rescue sinners.

Cousin Bertha and I did not like each other, but good manners and Christianity (hers) demanded of us a kind of steel-clad politeness.

There came a day, however, when my fifteen-year-old restraint developed explosive propensities. It was the day of my first date . . . a real date, I mean, with no brother tagging along to protect me.

Jack, tall and handsome as only a first date can be, was to call for me at seven-thirty. I was in a panic lest my blue silk blouse and black velvet skirt would not measure up to his well pressed serge. I had hurried home from school, put my hair up in curl-papers and was busy buffing my nails when the doorbell rang. It was Cousin Bertha. She often dropped in rather late in the afternoon knowing darn well my hospitable (and Anglican) mother would invite her to stay for dinner.

For once I peeled the potatoes and set the table willingly. Anything was better than having to entertain Cousin Bertha. She and mother chatted cosily in the parlor while I lined up the company cutlery beside fresh white linen napkins. Was it my fault the acoustics between parlor and diningroom were as perfect as any intentional eaves-dropper could wish? Cousin Bertha was talking about me.

"But Maudie, do you mean to tell me you are going to allow Helen to go out unchaperoned with a boy? You know, dear, she's prettier than I ever thought she would be. But she's such a child, so innocent, and good looks can be dangerous. My dear, such awful things can happen. Really Maudie, I simply cannot understand..."

Was there a slight note of resentment in mother's voice as she cut Cousin Bertha short?

"Now Bertha, don't be silly. Just because you've had dealings with bad and unfortunate girls you don't have to think of our Helen in that light. A girl brought up in a good home knows how to behave. And besides, Jack is a dear boy. We know his people. He comes of a highly respected family and I know very well he wouldn't .... he wouldn't .... but I suppose Helen isn't very grown up, is she .... and she knows so little about .... and you see I don't believe in telling young girls .... You've started me wondering if maybe I should try to persuade Helen to ...."

Mother's uncertainty was beginning to verge toward agreement with Cousin Bertha. Fortunately the click of father's key in the lock relieved her of having to make a decision.

"Hello dear, where are you?" he called as he came into the hall. "Oh hello Bertha, staying to dinner? And how's this wicked world treating you?" His tone was subtly jocular. Father, bless him, had saved my date.

The blue silk blouse did very well. We had a grand evening watching a junior athletic meet at the YMCA. (Poor Bertha, was there no place on earth safe for a young girl unchaperoned) The weather was fine so we walked home. What did kids of fifteen and eighteen talk about way back before the first world war? I don't remember but what I do remember vividly was the saying goodnight on the doorstep. There was awkwardness on my part and a strange reluctance to let him go with only "Thank you very much Jack. I've had a lovely time". I held out my hand. He took it in both of his and leaned toward me, his eyes bright and pleading. Why at that moment did Cousin Bertha's warning ring in my ears "My dear, such awful things can happen ".

As his arm went round my shoulders I drew back, trembling. Then pushing him from me I turned and with a haughty "goodnight" went in and firmly shut the door.

That was in September 1914. Three months later I heard that Jack had enlisted. I was hurt: he'd not called me since our date.

Two years went by. Other boys came and went and I did some growing up. Ironically, on the afternoon of the day I'd learned at school that Jack had been killed in action (there'd been a big push in France) Cousin Bertha came to tea. Coming in the back door with my arms full of schoolbooks I found mother in the kitchen. She was setting out cream and sugar and her Limoges cups and saucers on a silver tray. "Who's here?" I asked.

"Cousin Bertha is in the parlor. Come and have tea with us dear. It's a bit bleak out isn't it? A nice hot cup of tea will warm you." Little did she know how very bleak it was. My back was turned, she did not see my face. Something hard and tight was stuck in my throat. My legs felt cold and stiff. But two years of war had taught me something: here was a situation that had to be lived through.

She was sitting in mother's green satin chair with the light behind her but I could feel that sanctimonious smile. "Why Helen, you're prettier every time I see you and that blue dress just matches your eyes. Do all your girl friends wear their skirts that short, dear (mid-calf or longer) You know, Helen, pretty and good girls must be doubly careful about showing their ...."

I was staring at her. She must have seen the fury in my eyes, I hated her, would always hate her for having done me out of that kiss. And now Jack was dead. Slowly I went toward her but instead of taking her outstretched hand I looked right into her face and said "You are a nasty woman", then turned and walked out of the room. Cousin Bertha would never know how close she'd come to having her face slapped.

SHE PAINTS

by Helen Ball

It was an advertisement in a magazine, one of those exotic full page ads for cosmetics, that reminded me of my early experiments with powder and paint. In those days glamor was still just a word. It had not yet become standard equipment for the woman who hopes to win popularity, a job, a man or all three.

A drop of scent on the handkerchief or a light dusting of riz powder on the nose and chin was the accepted limit to which a nice woman could go. Rouging the cheeks was painting. No lady painted.

Riz powder came in chalk white and rose-pink. It was applied with a small square of chamois. Whether or not it was imported from France (probably most of it was) the spelling was always r-i-z and doubtless its Frenchness had a subtle sales value.

I remember an incident illustrating perfectly the stigma associated with the use of rouge. It was mother's day at home (every second Thursday from three to five) and I was being hopefully exposed to polite society. Dressed in my best white eyelet, I passed the tea and small cakes though I would have much preferred playing baseball with my brothers in the back yard.

A close family friend called rather late. Through the parlor window I watched her descent from a hired victoria. The horse was a glossy chestnut (how I longed to rush out and pat him) and a liveried coachman sat on the box.

She swept into the house, all ostrich feathers and black lace bosom. The earlier callers having left, there was no incentive for rigid formality and the conversation became casual and gossippy.

"Jenny, it's too bad you're so late," said my mother. "That little Mrs. Price was here. You know who I mean — the bride who's come to live across the street. Such a nice little thing and so pretty. Beautiful coloring."

"Beautiful coloring! " Jenny almost shouted. "Fanny, my dear, must you be so naive? Beautiful colouring indeed! She paints! ". Poor little Mrs. Price. Even her artistry couldn't save her.

That was still the attitude when in my middle teens, I suddenly stopped being a tomboy and became uncomfortably aware of my somewhat sallow complexion. It was a real cross until the day I discovered that my closest and dearest friend was rouging.

I loved her. I loved her pink cheeks. Who wanted to be a lady anyway? So it was pretty petite Phyllis who taught me how to stain my cheeks with, of all things, Christmas tissue paper. The technique was simple. One took a small piece of red tissue, moistened it with spit and then lightly applied a roundish spot of transparent color to each cheek. While still wet it had to be spread out quickly with the finger tips. The result was a surprisingly natural blush. If too vivid, it could be easily toned down with a piece of spit upon toilet paper.

It wasn't long before I learned to heighten the color of my lips by licking them, then, with a piece of red tissue between them, pressing them evenly and firmly together. Oh joy of joys, I began to feel beautiful. Oddly enough, mother made no comment. Was she still naive? I'll never know.

At eighteen I got my first job as a typist in a small business office in downtown Toronto. There were five girls on the staff and all but one used rouge and powder. I was beginning to feel that my red tissue technique was childishly unsophisticated when I happened upon a coupon in a magazine which read: "Detach here and send with 25c and you will receive (in a plain envelope) a generous sample of our new dry rouge". Off went the coupon with a precious quarter and instructions to send my sample to my office address.

In due time it arrived, and by observing the other girls I learned to make a passable success of using it, always scrubbing it off before leaving for home. Somehow it seemed less innocent than Christmas tissue.

One day when I was going directly from the office to Phyll's house for dinner, I was late finishing my work. When I got to our stuffy cubbyhole of a washroom which also served as a cloakroom, the other girls had gone. There on the shelf under a badly lit mirror was a box of riz powder, rose-pink. It belonged to a pleasant fair-skinned girl whose artistry with the ubiquitous chamois I admired. She'd spare me a little I felt sure. Here was my opportunity.

Ten minutes later I left the office and sprang the lock behind me. On the corner where I waited for a streetcar there was a restaurant with panels of mirror decorating its doorway.

Good heavens! Was that me? That mauve-faced hussy? That street walker?

I was a little hazy as to what a street walker actually was but instinct told me it was unwise to look like one. The office was locked. No going back to wash off that ghastly pink powder. Out came my hankie and I walked round the block scrubbing at my face. I squandered two cents on a newspaper and hid behind it on the streetcar.

Phyll's mother opened the door to me. "My dear, what's wrong? Are you ill? Have you a fever?" Her concern was genuine and it was more than I could take. With her arms round me I began to cry.

She was a much younger woman than my own mother and I knew it was she who introduced the red tissue technique to her daughter. My story was safe with her. She slathered my face with vaseline and in no time laughed me out of my unhappiness. I had learned the hard way that rose-pink powder was not for sallow skin. But I was well into my twenties before I acquired enough nerve to walk up to a beauty counter without first making sure none of mother's Jenny-friends were lurking nearby.

Periodicals began running ads for rouge and powder in shades never heard of before. Lip rouge appeared on the market in metal tubes – lipstick.

Quite nice women began carrying compacts (loose powder) in their handbags instead of soiled squares of chamois saturated with riz powder. Sales girls in the 5 and 10 and the big department stores were trained and eager to help the customer select the shade best suited to her complexion.

The time had come when even a lady could admit, at least to her intimates, that she painted. Glamor was stealthily coming into its own.

MODESTY AND MODERNITY

by Norman McPherson

Our generation has experienced the whole gamut of change in sexual matters from extreme prudery to extreme permissiveness. This astounding swing in attitude is amusingly illustrated by the two incidents which are narrated below.

Sixty years apart

The first episode is typically Victorian.

My mother, intent on her Saturday shopping, was hurrying along the main street on her way to the market, when she saw a youngster of about six years of age sitting on the curb. The child looked completely hopeless. She sat with her elbows on her knees and her head in her hands, staring at nothing. Carts and carriages clattered past on the cedar-block pavement, but she paid no attention. She looked so forlorn, with her long dress tucked around her ankles and her small sailor hat drooped over her nose, that you would think she had lost all interest in life.

For a moment my mother thought of stopping and asking the child what was wrong. But she was in a hurry and resisted the impulse. When she returned an hour later, with, among other things, two nice chickens which she had succeeded in buying for a quarter, she found the child still sitting on the curb, looking more disconcolate than ever.

Stopping beside her, my mother said, "My dear, you can't sit there all day. Why don't you run off home?"

"I can't."

"Why not?"

"I can't stand up."

"Are you hurt?"

"No."

"Why can't you stand up?"

The child looked at her miserably, and in a tone of voice that would have been appropriate for Lady MacBeth in the sleep-walking scene, she said, "My pants are falling off."

"Can't you pin them up?"

"No. 'Cause if I stand up, they'll fall down."

My mother didn't laugh. She sympathized with the child's predicament. She merely said, "You stay there, my dear, and I'll see what I can do."

Finding herself in front of a dry-goods store, she entered, and enlisted the services of two women who were shopping. The three stood around the unfortunate little girl, completely shielding her from view. Much relieved, the child stood up, and sure enough her pants fell to the ground. Hastily she picked them up and wrapped them in a newspaper, which one of the women handed her.

The proprieties had been observed and everybody was happy.

Today the child's excessive modesty seems merely amusing; but to the Edwardian it was only natural. Propriety must be maintained at all cost. If my mother had not intervened that child might well have sat there until after dark. A woman would go to extreme lengths to avoid any appearance of impropriety. Intimate garments such as corsets and panties, usually called drawers by girls of the period, were kept out of sight as much as possible, and were never referred to in mixed company. Most young women were embarrassed at having to hang their drawers (panties) out on the clothes-line to dry. One young woman whom my wife remembers solved this delicate problem with a good deal of ingenuity. She devised a way of stringing drawers on the clothes-line so that they looked exactly like pillow-slips.

When we were young modesty in women was still a virtue. The female form was hidden by enough fabric to clothe half a dozen women today. A woman might wear a bustle to accentuate the rotundity of her bottom, but she would be horrified at the idea of displaying the calf of her leg no matter how attractive it might be. Legs were not only concealed from view, they were not even referred to. One might speak without giving offence of a girl's lower limbs, but never of her legs.

So much for modesty.

The second incident is contemporary.

A young lady, a very attractive young lady, whose measurements were 36, 24, 36 or thereabouts, whose blond hair flowed down over her shoulders in wind-swept abandon, whose skin was soft and creamy, and whose red lips curled in a continual pout, lived with her widowed mother (grass not bereaved) in a cute little suburban bungalow.

In due time (that is when she was eighteen) the young lady became engaged to a young man who had some sort of job in some sort of office down town. It was a highly suitable engagement in every way. They were both deeply devoted to rock concerts, laughed at anything that was old-fashioned, and knew all about everything, except those erudite matters which are dealt with in books.

The wedding day was fixed for late June. But early in the month the mother took a sudden notion to fly off to the West Indies for three weeks' rest. Jamaica rum, she had always found, was exceedingly restful. She knew that things would become rather hectic around the date of the wedding, and she wanted to be completely relaxed.

On this particular afternoon, the charming young couple arrived at the bungalow about 5 o'clock. It was a warm day, and as usual they removed all unnecessary clothing. This included in the girl's case everything but the wrist-watch, and in the man's everything but the smile. You see, they held the opinion (an opinion which, according to certain clergymen, is widely held today) that the honeymoon should precede, not follow, the wedding.

163

Matters went forward merrily, until the girl suggested that they should go down to the games room for a drink.

Hand in hand they scampered down the stairs and burst into the games room, to find twenty or thirty of their friends waiting to give them a surprise party.

It was one of the most successful surprise parties ever held — that is, the intended recipients of the surprise were undeniably surprised, but they were no more surprised than were the supposed donors of the surprise party.

THE CORNER STORE
by Dora Macdonald

In those legendary days when coppers really bought something, and were not just used to make change from $10 when an article cost $9.98, I stood with two of my diminutive school-girl friends in front of a corner store looking wistfully in the grimy window. It was not a very big store. Just part of a private dwelling. On one side of the door was a box filled with cracked ice and lake trout, which had just arrived that morning from Lake Huron. On the other side stood a bushel basket of potatoes, many of them sprouting.

"Gee! " I said. "Let's hope it isn't Mr. Fleury who waits on us."

"He's awfully stingy, "said Alice.

"And kind of crabby, " added Mabel.

I was a small-boned little imp with blue eyes and blond hair. My aunts, dear souls, thought that I was pretty. But they made a fuss over all children. Alice was tall for her age, and was sometimes inclined to put on airs. Her head was too big for her body — or rather, her body had not yet grown to match the size of her head. This incongruity made her look more mature than she was. Mabel was plump and giggly. When something delighted her, she wriggled all over and hugged herself gleefully. Alice was the best dressed of the three. She had on a pale blue gingham dress, with a dark blue sash and a blue ribbon in her hair. Mabel and I wore serviceable cotton print dresses with no special adornment, except droopy hair ribbons.

Among us we had two coppers to buy globe chocolates. My father had given me the coppers for helping my mother with the dishes all the previous week. If Mrs. Fleury waited on us it would be all right. She was a plump jolly woman who always called me dearie, and gave us several chocolates, no matter how few coppers we had. But Mr. Fleury was different. Squinting through his steel-rimmed spectacles, he carefully counted out one chocolate for each copper, no more. To be sure they were

A corner store

very big chocolates, much bigger than modern chocolates. But it would be awfully hard to divide two chocolates equally among three girls.

Mr. Fleury was thin, and stooped, and always wore a white apron. "I wish we had three cents," said Mabel regretfully.

"My mother didn't have any coppers, so she couldn't give me any," said Alice. "I mean," she added hastily, "she had lots of money, but no coppers."

Alice's father worked in a bank, and in those days banks did not pay very high salaries. But the family felt that his position required them to put up a good front. In public they always pretended that they had plenty of money.

"Your mother might have given you five cents," I said. "Then we could have had all the chocolates we wanted."

"Nobody ever gives anybody five cents," said Alice haughtily. "You know that."

"Except on your birthday," declared Mabel. "My aunt always gives me one cent for every year I am old. Last birthday she gave me six cents."

Other children were passing on their way to school, and we knew that we would have to hurry, if we did not want to be late. We entered the store to the jingle of the spring bell above the door, and, much to our relief, we found Mrs. Fleury busy behind the counter. She gave us a whole bag of chocolates, a small bag to be sure, but it contained enough chocolates so that each of us could have two. We ate one immediately, relishing each bite properly, and kept the other for recess.

Several weeks later, when the weather had become oppressively hot and the summer holidays were approaching, Mabel, Alice, and I stood in front of the same store. But we were not looking in the store window. In fact, we were huddled on the other side of the board walk talking in whispers. Something had happened which we did not understand.

"I've got three cents," I said. "But we can't buy any chocolates. The store is closed."

"Why is it closed?" asked Mabel. "It isn't Sunday".

"Somebody is deaded, silly," said Alice. Didn't you see the black crepe on the door? I mean the other door, not the store door."

"Gee! I hope it's old Mr. Fleury," said Mabel. "It would serve him right for being so stingy."

"You mustn't say bad things," I admonished her, "about somebody who is dead."

"We don't know he's dead," said Mabel defensively. "We only hope he is."

But when we got home from school we learned that it was not Mr. Fleury who had died, but his wife. We gathered round a swing in Mabel's backyard, and in subdued voices discussed what had happened. This was the first time we had experienced death so close to home. Mabel, who was not only giggly but very sentimental, several times wiped tears from her eyes.

"I'm sorry she's dead," said Alice. "Now we'll never get all the chocolates we want."

"You shouldn't think of yourself when someone has died," I said in my most superior manner. "You should just think how sad it is to be lying there in the coffin, and not able to talk or run or anything. And everybody crying because you are dead."

In those days I was such a self-righteous little prig that it is a wonder somebody didn't wring my neck. But my companions didn't mind. Youngsters are used to being set right.

"Do you suppose old Mr. Fleury will be sorry?" Alice asked, not a bit ashamed of herself for thinking of the chocolates.

"Of course he'll be sorry," said Mabel. "My Uncle Timothy was terribly upset when Aunt Martha died. He only ate one poached egg for breakfast that morning."

"Every man is upset when his wife dies," I said, proud of myself for saying something really important. "Everybody knows that."

"When Aunt Martha died everybody sent flowers," said Mabel. "You could scarcely see the coffin, 'cause it was all covered up with flowers."

Mention of flowers set us all thinking. Nobody said anything for several minutes. We just thought and thought. Then Alice, who was the practical one, came up with a brilliant suggestion.

"We must send flowers to Mrs. Fleury's funeral," she declared. "We are sort of friends of hers, 'cause she gave us so many chocolates."

"But we have no money," Mabel and I immediately protested. "And flowers cost an awful lot of money when you buy them at the store."

"We don't need money, sillies," Alice said. "We can gather the flowers ourselves. There is a rosebush by our front steps. It's awfully prickly. But we can cut the flowers off with scissors."

"Uncle Timothy has lots of flowers in his garden," said Mabel, warming to the idea. "I'm sure he wouldn't mind if we picked some."

With enthusiasm we went about collecting flowers. We gathered everything that bloomed; lilacs and moss roses, peonies and bleeding hearts, irises and buttercups, together with some oxeye daisies and a purple thistle which we found in a vacant lot. It was a huge and conglomerate bouquet, so large that Alice had to hold it in her arms, not her hands. We tied it with a piece of ribbon which Mabel found in her mother's workbasket. None of us knew how to tie a bowknot. But we tucked in the ends of the ribbon, and it didn't look so bad.

Well satisfied with our effort, we set out for Mr. Fleury's residence.

The main door of the dwelling, the door on which the crepe was hung, was at the side of the building, and was overhung by a climbing vine. Timidly we knocked and waited, just a little frightened at our own boldness.

After a long pause the door opened and Mr. Fleury stood there frowning.

"Be off with you," he said crossly. "I can't be bothered with you at a time like this."

Mabel and I would have scampered off home immediately. We were both rather timid, and were easily overawed by older people. But Alice, who carried the bouquet, had more assurance.

"Here are some flowers for Mrs. Fleury's funeral," she said, holding out the cumbersome bouquet. "We're awfully sorry that she died."

She spoke hurriedly, as if she were out of breath. But she succeeded in uttering her little speech with childish sincerity.

For some minutes the old man looked at her in puzzlement, fumbling with his watch chain. Then his eyes filled with tears and his lips trembled.

"Thank you, thank you kindly," he said. "I'll put them on the coffin where everyone can see them."

Ever after that Mr. Fleury smiled at us when we went into the store. He continued to count out the chocolates, one for each cent. But we did not mind. Was it because our childish gesture of kindness had formed a bond of understanding between us? Or was it because we had seen tears in the old man's eyes? Whatever it was, we no longer thought that he was stingy. Just careful, as everyone must be.

WOMEN IN REVOLT

by Norman McPherson

The Victorian Era was characterized by stability; the present age by turmoil and stress. The period which we are picturing was a transition period between the two extremes. Though it still retained a high degree of social and economic stability, there were stirrings of unrest. Workers were beginning to feel that they were not being treated fairly in the distribution of the nation's wealth, and were organizing trade unions. But that is a story in itself. What we are concerned with here is the revolt of women against the stuffy Victorian family ethics, and the limitations imposed on their activities outside the home by age-old tradition.

The Victorian family, whose essential character was based on ancient Roman law, was a marvelous structure, solid, enduring, and productive. To most people of the time it seemed to conform, not only to natural law, but to the will of God. The man, being masterful and mentally superior to the woman (Comment: Oh yeh!) was eminently equipped to be head of the household and to manage the financial affairs of the family. The woman, on the other hand, though not so clever as the man (Comment: Poppycock!) was loving and devoted and obviously intended by God to function as wife and mother in the home.

When the man was wise and the woman was humble and devoted, the scheme worked admirably. The story goes that one day the Prince Consort was in a certain room, the door to which happened to be locked. The queen came to the door and wished to gain entrance. She knocked.

"Who's there? " cried the Prince.

"The Queen of England," answered Victoria with dignity.

Once more the Prince said, "Who's there? "

Again the answer came, "The Queen of England."

But he would not let her in until she replied humbly, "Your loving wife."

Head of the household

No marriage could be happier than the marriage of Queen Victoria to her adored Prince Albert. It served as a model for all married couples in the British Empire. Queen Victoria herself, it might be noted in passing, was steadfastly opposed to any change in the dependent status of women.

In the traditional marriage service the groom was required to say, "With all my worldly goods I thee endow." But that of course was for the birds. Everybody knew that women, silly creatures, just became confused when they were forced to deal with money matters. (Comment: Confused my eye! Look who's talking!) When a woman married, even if she possessed considerable wealth, she did not need to worry her poor head any further about worldly goods. All her property passed immediately to the control of her husband. (Comment: The dirty dogs! They took all her money, and made her do all the dirty work!) In England this inequity was corrected in the Married Women's Property Act of 1882. By the provisions of this act a married woman was entitled to own, acquire, or dispose of real or personal property as if she were a single woman. In due time most of the provinces of Canada (Quebec's civil law is different from that of the other provinces) enacted similar legislation.

Though such a measure was a step in the right direction, it did little to alter the general masculine attitude towards women. Most men still felt that women should confine their interest and their energy to domestic matters, while men looked after the broader and more complex affairs of the nation. Above all women should keep out of politics.

In Canada, Nellie McClung was the best known suffragette of the period. Recently a postage stamp bearing her portrait was issued in her honor. But Marion Collins (wife of John who wrote "Be it Ever So Humble"), remembers vividly living as a child across the street from Nellie in Winnipeg. She also remembers vividly that her father cherished a deep and abiding hatred for everything Nellie stood for. He used to growl, "If that damned woman would stay home and look after her unruly brats instead of gadding about the country talking nonsensical blither, she might be of some use in this world."

And that is what many men honestly felt deep in their hearts. At one point Nellie's own brother advised her strongly to give up public speaking, and confine herself to her home and her family. It is not easy to dispel such firmly embedded prejudices.

In marriage the woman's chief function was of course the production of offspring with clock-like regularity. With females constructed as they were, nobody could doubt that such was God's intent. (Comment: except Malthus.) One of our members recalls a Mrs. Rolph, a charwoman with a ne'er-do-well husband, who, when asked about her family, would reply "There be twenty-one. Ten on earth, and eleven in heaven, God bless their souls!" What modern woman, with her head full of unwomanly matters, could hope to equal that high degree of productivity?

Besides producing children the wife was expected to manage her household so efficiently that when her lord and master returned from his daily toil (Comment: or betting on the races!) he would find a haven of rest and comfort. For amusement the housewife could indulge in social activities. Receiving callers, and returning calls. Giving euchre parties. Or acting as chaperone at a ball put on in the armories by the officers of the local militia regiment. (Comment: While her husband, gay dog, danced with all the pretty girls.)

The Victorian family fostered two types of women, the noble woman who sacrificed everything for her husband and her family, and the vapid, brainless type of woman. A. P. Herbert with sardonic humor described the sort of girls he liked: "I like 'em fluffy. No brains at all. Just fluffy! " (Comment: God preserve us from fluffy girls, and noble women!) The men of the period did not approve of independent women, who wished to build a career for themselves outside the home. Nor did they think too highly of educated women, who took an intelligent interest in the issues of the day.

The Lib-type women of today have a term for those men who claim masculine superiority. They call them male chauvinists. But that is a poor term to describe the typical Victorian male. Men of that period put women on a pedestal. They wrote romantic tales about the beautiful maiden whose hand was ultimately won by the gallant hero; and they venerated motherhood. They believed that women were too delicate, too sensitive to engage in the grubby matter of earning a living. (Comment: Except in some menial capacity, like scrubbing the floors of an office building at night.) They held that women were so wrapped up in being wives and mothers that they could not possibly have any opinions worth considering on such mundane matters as politics. (Comment: Baloney!) And they treated women with extreme politeness. (Comment: Bah! Who needs it?) But the Victorian male had one great weakness. With sublime egotism, he never looked at things from the woman's point of view. He never asked, what do women hope to get out of life? But always, how best can women contribute to man's well-being?

All through life they depended on their womenfolk. When they were boys, their mothers loved them, cared for them, and protected them from harm. The girls of the family were expected to look after themselves, and sometimes to wait on their brothers. (Comment: My grandfather expected his daughters to polish their

A Victorian matron

brothers' boots.) When they were married, their wives looked after their every desire, and provided for their every comfort. And when they were old, their daughters, not their sons, saw to it that they ended their days in a dignified manner.

The Victorian male enjoyed a cosy existence. Is it any wonder that the old dears tried desperately to preserve the status quo? Is it any wonder that they resented the activities of those restless females like Emmeline Pankhurst who so vociferously claimed that women had rights as well as men? To them it appeared that such women were behaving in a manner contrary to the Divine Will, and they quoted St. Paul to prove it.

It was by their patriotic activities during the First World War that women ultimately won some degree of independence. During the war they worked on the farms to produce food; and they worked in the factories to produce munitions. In Canada they were granted the right to vote in provincial elections, first in Manitoba in 1916, in Ontario in 1917, and in federal elections in 1918.

But it was in the years immediately preceding the war that the groundwork was laid for the most significant social revolution of all time. It was a revolution in the relative status of men and women in marriage and in the community. The attempt to reach a state of equality, a state of equilibrium is still going on. Where we are at the present time can best be learned by reading "The Report of the Royal Commission on the Status of Women in Canada" published in 1970. The story about Fanny which follows this article illustrates in dramatic form the attitude towards women in the mid-nineties of last century. Fanny's case was extreme, but it was by no means unusual. Fanny was the victim of those traditional masculine attitudes which the new women of the twentieth century so violently revolted against, attitudes which women of today find it difficult to comprehend.

One should, however, make an emphatic statement at this point. It is the custom today to deride, as we have been doing, anything that in the least smacks of Victorianism. In the main such criticism is justified. Other times, other customs. The social upheaval which we have been hinting at was overdue and inevitable. As conditions altered with the dawn of the twentieth century, the out-moded family ethics which had prevailed from Roman times became unbearable to some women, and irksome to many. But when we criticize, we should be fair. We may laugh at the quaint social customs of a period that is long departed. We may laugh at the excessive politeness that prevailed at that time. But it is undoubted that those social customs and that politeness added a graciousness to life which we cannot hope to emulate in our brash and uninhibited suburbs of today. And it is equally undoubted that many married women in the nineties lived happy and rewarding lives. The typical housewife of the period was a sturdy, hard-working, warm-hearted woman, who was perfectly contented with her lot in life. When love is in the home, what does it matter who controls the purse strings? When each is there to help the other, what does it matter who rules the roost? Most of us today can remember our grandmothers with love and genuine respect, and we can not help wondering if the young married women of today, with all their vaunted freedom, will deserve such admiration from their grandchildren when they grow old. (Comment: What about their footloose granddaddies?)

But at the turn of the century women were becoming restless. They wanted the right to count for something, not only in the home, but on the national scene. They wanted more opportunities for earning a living. They saw no reason why they should not become doctors, or lawyers, or successful businesswomen. Before 1895, very few women sought higher education; but many of the girls we went to high school with went on to the university, or took special training as nurses, teachers, or stenographers. Judge Emily Murphy, whose pen-name was Janey Canuck, wrote: "The only really contented women are those who have both a home and a profession." It was our generation which was responsible for producing the first examples of what are now regarded as the modern woman. Among the many women in Canada who fought for women's rights, the most colorful and the most energetic was Nellie McClung. She was a remarkable woman, who deserves a distinguished place in the annals of our country.

NELLIE McCLUNG

Nellie McClung's life is rich with the drama and romance of Canadian history. She lived two lives: first, as a young woman fighting the hardships and privations of a pioneer farm in Ontario, and later in a log cabin in Manitoba when that prairie province was receiving its first real influx of settlers; and secondly, as a prominent new woman of the twentieth century, a woman of the world, successful, politically aware, a popular novelist and accomplished public speaker, a woman who had made her mark in the complex and sophisticated society of the modern age.

She wrote of her early life: "We lived a mile from Chatsworth ... in a stony part of the County of Grey. The stones lay over our farm like flocks of sheep." John Mooney, an Irishman, had cleared the land of the primeval forest, and was doing his best by endless toil to squeeze out a living from the unpromising soil for himself and his family. Her mother, whose maiden name was Letitia McCurdy, came from Dundee, Scotland. She was a typical Victorian pioneer, sturdy, resourceful, hard-working, courageous, far too busy being a wife and a mother to think of women's rights, much too fully occupied with the endless chores of a farmer's wife to bother her head about politics. One winter before Nellie was born, her mother was forced to deal with incredible difficulties. Her husband was laid up for weeks with what was called bronchitis.

"The snow was so deep," Nellie wrote, "that for three weeks no sleigh could get through, and she was there alone, with a sick man, and three small children, one a baby a month old, and ten head of stock to feed and water."

When the men (her oldest brother and her father) found it impossible to do more than scrape out a living from their stony land, they pulled up stakes and moved to Manitoba. They travelled by wagon to Owen Sound, by boat to Duluth (the CPR was not yet completed) and by train to St. Boniface,

Nellie sets out for school

where they arrived at night. Since the ferry-boat ran only in the day time, they loaded themselves and their belongings into a big scow, and were rowed across the river to Winnipeg proper.

Nellie's oldest brother, Will, had gone out the previous year to survey the land and make preparations for their coming. He met them in Winnipeg, and drew a plan of the block of land he had claimed for them, eight hundred acres of rich, black, loam, one hundred and eighty miles south of Winnipeg. The story of their stay near Winnipeg while Will and her father built a log cabin, of their journey to their new home with all their belongings piled high on two ox-drawn wagons, and of that first bitterly cold winter in their draughty new abode reads like a script for a movie. Slowly the district was filled with other settlers, a church was built, and then a school.

By that time, Nellie, the youngest in a family of six, was ten years old. She had never been to school, and could not read. Wearing a rough homespun dress made by her mother, copper-toed shoes too big for her (newspapers were stuffed in the toes to make them fit) with her hair cut short, no hair ribbon, she walked the two or three miles to school on the opening day. The teacher was a man. When he called her to his desk, she confessed with deep foreboding that she could not read though she was ten years old.

"Good! " said the teacher reassuringly. "A very good time to begin school; you'll be reading in three months."

Having once started her education, Nellie progressed rapidly. Before many years had passed, she wrote her high school leaving examination at Brandon. Like a good many girls before and after her, she was fearful that she had failed in algebra. After some weeks, however, she received a post-card from the government carrying what she described as "the sweetest words I had ever seen on paper: 'Having passed the recent second class Teachers' Examination you are eligible to attend ... the Normal School in Winnipeg.'"

It was while she was teaching in a rural school that she resolved to become a writer. She admired Dickens, and she wanted to write about underprivileged people as he had done. From her slender salary she bought books and more books, among them Ruskin's "Sesame and Lilies". Ruskin was a master of the English language. "I would hammer out my education," she wrote, "on the hard anvil of life. I would mine for words as eagerly as any miner ever dug for gold."

Finally she got a position teaching in a town called Manitou, where she boarded with the Methodist minister and his family. Manitou was a typical booming western town.

"We had no telephones, picture-shows, radios, phonographs, daily papers or lending libraries. We made our own fun."

The town had a weekly newspaper called "The Mercury". On a certain occasion one of the stores advertised, "Three men killed in the jam at our Saturday's bargains! "

The rival store immediately replied: "There are no dead men in our jam."

This is typical western humor. If you are going to exaggerate, give them a whopper!

The minister's oldest son, Wes, became the local druggist, and in due time he and Nellie were married. As Nellie put it, "We did not always agree but he was a fair fighter, and I knew I would rather fight with him than agree with anyone else."

They were very happy living in a four-roomed apartment over the drug store. Nellie was a devoted wife and mother, but she saw so much suffering among less fortunate people that she was impelled to do something about it. She could not be happy herself, if those round about her were in misery. She became a crusader; a crusader for the rights of the downtrodden, the impoverished, the over-worked. She observed that a good deal of the misery among women was caused by drunkenness among the men. Her first public speech was an address of welcome to delegates of the Women's Christian Temperance Union who were holding a conference in Manitou. She knew that much of the drunkenness was due to boredom, to what she called the "grey monotony" of life on the prairie. With her usual originality, she did not rant about the evils of the demon rum. Instead she painted a glowing picture of how life could be exciting and happy without the use of alcohol.

Nellie followed a good rule when she was required to make a speech. If she had nothing to say she bought a fancy new dress, made a special trip to the hairdresser, had her nails polished; in short made herself as glamorous as possible. But if she really had something to say she didn't care how she was dressed.

It was while the McClungs were living in Manitou that Nellie wrote her first story. At the instigation of her mother-in-law, a woman whom she loved and admired, she entered a short story in a competition sponsored by "Collier's " magazine. This was in 1902. Her story did not win a prize, but the Editor thought highly enough of it to write her a letter. He said that the story was too juvenile for their purposes, but he described it as "a delightful story, with humor and originality."

For some reason she did not do anything about the manuscript for some time. Finally, it came to the attention of the Brigg's Publishing Company, and they advised her to expand it into a book. This she did, and it was finally published in 1908, under the title "Sowing Seeds in Danny". It immediately became a best-seller in Canada, and did very well in the United States. Following that success she wrote several more novels, and two or three other books mostly autobiographical.

After fifteen years in Manitou, Nellie's husband sold his drug store, and accepted an insurance agency in Winnipeg, where they bought a house. It was not long until Nellie's bubbling effervescence asserted itself among the women of the city. A visit of Emmeline Pankhurst encouraged the women to organize. Their immediate concern was to improve the lot of women doing piece work in small factories. The conditions in which these unfortunate women worked were appalling — low wages, long hours, filthy surroundings. They persuaded Sir Rodmond Roblin, the Premier, to accompany them on a visit to some of the plants. He was horrified at what he saw. "I never knew that such hell-holes existed! " he declared.

The main interest of the women, however, their over-riding desire, was to get the vote. They organized a campaign throughout the province, and Nellie became an aggressive suffragette. Her saving grace as a crusader, what saved her from becoming a fanatical militant, was her sense of humor.

Sir Rodmond Roblin and his Conservative government were violently opposed to anything so unprecedented as women's suffrage.

Inspired by Nellie, the women decided to gain their point, not by chaining themselves to iron fences, not by throwing themselves in front of horses, nor by going on hunger strikes, but by laughter. Ridicule they believed would be more deadly than violence. They formed a mock parliament to discuss the question, should men be given the vote? The day before the performance Nellie and two or three other women visited the legislature and put in a petition requesting the right to vote. Sir Rodmond replied. He was a solemn and pompous orator of the old school. Nellie, who was to act as Premier in the mock parliament, noted every gesture, every tone of voice, every condescending phrase.

Next night the theatre was packed. The mock parliament proceeded with great dignity. Page boys ran about delivering messages, some members read newspapers while others delivered dreary speeches, and Nellie aped the Premier to a tee, reducing his pompous oratory to pompous humbug. The theatre rocked with laughter, the newspapers reported the performance at length, and at the next election the Conservatives went down to ignominous defeat.

The women of Manitoba got the vote in 1916, the first in Canada.

Some time later the McClungs moved to Edmonton. In due time Nellie became a member of the provincial legislature of Alberta. It was while the McClungs lived in Edmonton that Nellie achieved her best remembered success as a crusader. The British North American Act, Canada's constitution, failed to recognize women as "persons". In company with Judge Emily Murphy, the first woman judge in Canada, and three other prominent women, Nellie fought the issue through the Privy Council in Great Britain, and won their contention. As a result of their efforts, women are now recognized as "persons" and can legally hold public office. The names of these illustrious women are inscribed on a plaque in the foyer of the Senate Chamber in Ottawa.

From here on Nellie's story reads like the story of other prominent women in Canada. She travelled much, she spoke often, she never gave up crusading, and she died during the Second World War.

FANNY

If Fanny had been able to deck herself out when she was young, she would have been as attractive as other young girls in the neighborhood. But with years of hard work, and a father who did not believe in spending money on female frivolity, she looked at thirty-four as if she were forty. Her forehead was furrowed, her green eyes were sad and dreamless, and her thin lips seldom smiled. Her hair, which was of an indeterminate color difficult to name, was parted in the middle and gathered in a knot at the back of her head. As she sat with her hands in her lap, listening to the lawyer's monotonous voice, she looked as if she were impatient to be up and doing.

The lawyer had driven out from town that morning. He was a wise old owl with a big paunch and a lugubrious face, and he knew what he was doing. He wasn't going to miss the chance of sitting down to one of Fanny's excellent meals. Fanny's cooking was famous throughout the whole county. How she managed with the dilapidated old stove, a relic of pioneer days, nobody knew. But she could work marvels with a cut of pork, and her home-made bread and her pies always took the prizes at the fall fair.

When the lawyer had arrived, her two older brothers had been working in the fields (the youngest was a cripple) and Fanny had herself unhitched his old nag, and had seen her properly tied up in a vacant stall.

The lawyer's voice droned on, pausing every now and then to make a long-winded explanation of some legal phraseology.

Old man McClintock, Fanny's father, had been one of the richest men in Elgin County. A hard man and tight with his money, he had accumulated a substantial bank balance, no mean feat on a farm in the later years of last century. His sons had toiled for him like hired hands though he had paid them no wages. The neighbors all believed that he had killed his wife by over work. Fanny had wanted to attend high school and become a teacher. But when her mother had died, gasping her life away on a bitterly cold night when the snow was piled high about the house, Fanny, then a girl in her teens, had been forced to take over the household management.

"I bequeath to my oldest son, John..." the lawyer's voice droned on.

There had been a time when the neighbors thought that Fanny might marry. A farmer's son had been seen to wait for her at the church door more than once. He had even been known to call at her home. But it is difficult to pay court to a girl who is milking cows, hoeing weeds from the vegetable patch, churning butter, or feeding the pigs. Even the most ardent suitor might become discouraged in such circumstances, and this young man had been at best only lukewarm. In the end he had ceased to come round, and finally had married someone else.

"To my second son, Hamish, I bequeath..." the lawyer continued tonelessly.

Fanny was glad that her youngest brother, the cripple, was to have some money. When she had found that she herself could not continue at school, she had resolved that he at any rate should get a good education. In the mild weather the boy had been able to struggle to school on crutches. But in winter she had gone with him, often carrying him piggyback through the deepest snowdrifts. But it was no use. He had no relish for book learning. He had quit school to follow his natural bent, the construction of ingenious devices that were useful around the farm. His father had set up a work-bench for him in the unused parlor. The room had been properly furnished when the old man had married. But it had not been used as a parlor for as long as Fanny could remember. The paper was peeling off the walls and the carpet was mildewed. But there Duncan would hammer and saw contentedly most of the day. With this money, Fanny thought, he could now buy all the tools he had always longed for.

"To St. James' Church I leave fifty dollars to be applied towards the purchase of an organ," the lawyer concluded. And he added with obvious self-satisfaction, "There, in my opinion, is a fine last will and testament, fair and just to all concerned,"

"Here! Here! " said Fanny's brothers in chorus.

Fanny did not say anything. She had not even been mentioned in the will. She just got to her feet and set about washing up the pile of dirty dishes that had been left from dinner.

That night, after she had blown out the lamp and crawled into her hard bed, Fanny did a lot of thinking. She was not surprised that she had not been mentioned in the will. It was the custom to leave everything to the men of the family, and to expect them to look after their sisters. In her case this would mean that she would be permitted to slave for her three brothers as she had slaved for her father, until, like her mother, she was ready to be carried to the family burying place under the tall elms near the willow-lined creek that crossed the back of the farm.

She lay there thinking and listening to the night sounds — the heavy breathing of her two older brothers in the next room, the distant barking of a neighbor's dog, the rustle of leaves in the maple tree which stood outside the window.

It must have been nearly midnight when she finally dropped off to sleep. But she had made up her mind. She knew what she was going to do.

Fanny got up earlier than usual the following morning, finished the early morning chores, gave the boys their breakfast, and cleaned up the kitchen. She then went up to her bedroom and changed into her Sunday dress ,It was a purple delaine that she herself had made. Once it had been pretty, but now it was badly faded. From under the mattress she extracted thirty-eight dollars which over the years she had saved from her egg money, and tucked it in her purse. Next she got out an old carpet-bag and packed it with her few belongings. This done, she put on her bonnet and descended to the kitchen.

She knew that a neighbor, Joe McDermid, was driving into town that morning with a load of potatoes. But he would not be along for another hour. To fill in the time she went out to the back porch and stood looking over the scene which she knew so well. Her eyes rested on the well built barns, the neat sheds, the carefully pruned orchard. Over the wood lot a flock of blackbirds wheeled and swooped preparatory to leaving for the south. John was ploughing in the ten acre field. The cows were grazing peacefully on the pasture land. Hamish she knew was cleaning out the stable. Behind her in the house she could hear Duncan hammering at his work-bench. It all seemed so familiar, so much a part of herself, that she found it hard to realize that she was leaving it for good.

As he stood motionless and pensive, the old collie dog (the younger dog was off in the field with John) came up to her and licked her hand.

Fanny was not given to tears. But her eyes welled up and everything became blurred and indistinct.

She picked up her carpet-bag and went slowly down to the road, followed by the old collie.

Joe McDermid reined his team to a halt when he saw her waiting by the roadside.

"You looking for a ride, Miss Fanny? "

"Yes. Are you going into town? "

"I am. And you're welcome to come along, if so be you want to."

Fanny threw her carpet-bag into the wagon and climbed up beside Joe. The old collie barked twice, and they lumbered off down the road.

Joe was very much puzzled. What could Fanny want in town? He waited patiently for her to make some explanation, and from time to time he glanced at her out of the corner of his eye. Her weather-beaten face was hard and set, and her eyes were staring straight ahead. At last his curiosity got the better of him.

"You got some sick relative in town, Miss Fanny? "

He knew perfectly well that the McClintocks had no relative in town, but he hoped that the question would start her talking.

"No."

"Maybe you're going to visit some friends for a few days? To kind of forget about your father's death and all? "

"No."

They drove on for a mile or two in silence. Joe couldn't understand the situation.

"Tain't none of my business, Miss Fanny. But why the heck are you going to town? "

"I'm leaving the farm, Joe. For good."

188

He looked at her as if he thought she was out of her head.

"Do your brothers know about this, Miss Fanny? "

"Joe," she said, "I clean forgot to let them know. When you get back from town will you drop in and tell them?"

"I sure will, Miss Fanny. But believe me, it will be an awful shock to them."

For the first time Fanny smiled, but her smile was as bleak as a gleam of sunlight in a wintry sky. Secretly she was enjoying the picture of her brothers' bewilderment when they learned that she was gone. Maybe that would teach them that women should not be regarded as mere conveniences.

"Yes Joe," she agree, "It will be a shock to them all right."

Nothing more was said until they got to town. He let her off on the main street near the market. When he handed her the carpet-bag he said, "Well, Miss Fanny, I hope you know what you're doing. But you're a strange woman. I can't make you out - leaving a good home and all. But good-bye and good luck."

Fanny registered at an hotel near the market. The proprietor himself showed her to her room. But she was appalled at the rate — a dollar and a half a day! She thought it was robbery. When she had left her bag in the room, she went out to look for lodging in a private house. She was lucky. Not far from the hotel she came on a small frame house with a sign in the window which read, "Room and Board". She was admitted by a dowdy woman with protuberant eyes and a discontented mouth. The room was small and the furniture poor, but Fanny was used to that sort of thing. After some haggling it was settled that she would have the room and breakfast for three dollars a week.

Fanny's next task was to find work. She had vague ideas of starting a boarding house or setting herself up as a dressmaker. But such schemes would have to wait until she had saved some money. In the meantime she thought that it would be easy to find work as a housekeeper. But she was mistaken. For days she wandered up one street and down another enquiring at any likely looking house. October slipped into November, and the autumn gales soughed through the leafless trees and drove scuds of rain down the cheerless streets. In spite of her thriftiness Fanny's money was soon spent. Her boarding-house mistress became querulous, then waspish, and finally downright hostile.

Each day she would greet Fanny at the door with the question, "Where's my money? " At last Fanny could stand it no longer. She packed up her bag and left. But where she was going she had no idea.

It was a bitterly cold day, with overcast sky and the wind out of the east.Wearily she plodded from door to door asking for work, any kind of work. But it was no use. Seeing her old carpet-bag and her bedraggled appearance, people seemed to think that she was some sort of disreputable tramp, and often slammed the door in her face.

With the approach of darkness the rain came down, a chill biting rain that lashed at her face and trickled down her neck. The lights in the houses along the way went out one by one, as if extinguished by the downpour, until only the occasional gas lamp at a street corner was left to blink drearily through the night. Fanny felt like an outcast, rejected and homeless.

Some time towards midnight, in the light of a street lamp, she caught sight of a park bench. She knew where she was now. This was the park behind the courthouse. Wearily she went over and sat down. She was so miserable that her mind was numb. If anything, the rain was getting worse. She could see it beating on the boardwalk under the street lamp, and drifting away in dissolving clouds of mist. She wondered if she had the strength to walk the long eight miles back to the farm. Once she got to her feet, picked up her bag, and made as if to start. But something restrained her. Was it her pride? Was it grim determination that once having put her hand to the plow she would not look back? Whatever it was, she dropped her bag and sat down again on the bench.

It must have been an hour later that she became aware of slow regular footsteps approaching down the street. When a dim figure appeared under the street lamp, she could see that it was a policeman. He came on slowly until he was opposite to her on the sidewalk, and there he stopped. Shielding his eyes against the rain with his hand, he peered at her through the darkness. Then he came over towards her.

"Come on," he said harshly. "Get moving. You can't loaf there, you know."

"I have no place to go," said Fanny.

"Sorry lady. But you can't stay here. No loiterers after curfew. Those are my orders."

She picked up her bag and followed him back to the sidewalk. Though he had to obey orders, he was not at heart an unkindly man. He felt sorry for Fanny and proceeded to question her further. But he was interrupted by the clip-clop of a horse's hooves. A light carriage drove up and stopped. In it was a bulky figure of a man huddled against the rain.

"Is that you, Donovan? " said the man in a gruff voice.

"Yes Doctor. You're out late in this cheerless night."

"Oh, I was just ushering another infant into this bleak and inhospitable world. How's your own youngster? "

"Mighty bad with the croup last night, Doctor. But with the daylight she seemed better."

"Well, I'll be along in the morning to have a look at her," said the doctor. Then he noticed Fanny. "Who's that woman? "

"Don't know. I found her sitting on a park bench."

"Send her home. This is no night for anyone to be out, man or woman."

"She said she has no home to go to, Doctor."

"Nonsense. Everybody has a home."

"Not her, Doctor. At least, that's what she says."

"Well, take her to the jail and lock her up. If she stays here she'll get pneumonia."

He flicked the reins and drove off. But when he was a few yards away he stopped and called over his shoulder, "Can the woman work, Donovan? "

It was Fanny who answered.

"I can do any kind of work that's fit for a woman, and some that isn't."

"Come on then."

Fanny hurried along the sidewalk and climbed into the carriage beside the doctor. She helped him stable his mare, wiping her down with a big rag, while the doctor filled her manger with hay.

In the house she got her first proper look at the doctor. Doctor Van Buskirk was a stocky man, partly bald but with a neatly trimmed beard. Though his manner was gruff, he had a comforting habit of dropping his head and looking over his pince-nez glasses at the person he was talking to. His gray eyes were thoughtful and kindly. He refused to talk to Fanny until she had slept. But in the morning he agreed to pay her twelve dollars a month to act as housekeeper.

The doctor's wife was a hypochondriac who suffered much from migraine. She would always stay in bed with the blinds down and the curtains drawn until late in the morning. Sometimes she would stay there all day. There were three children, two boys and a girl, who needed constant attention, especially the youngest.

Fanny's duties as housekeeper were multifarious. She had to prepare all the meals, and keep the large house swept, scrubbed, and dusted. She was continually taking trays upstairs for Mrs. Van Buskirk, or giving her medicine, or getting cold compresses for her head. She had to see that the children were washed and dressed and off to school on time. In addition to these household chores, she had the doctor's office to attend to — answering knocks at the door, taking messages for the doctor, and handing out bottles of medicine.

She sent a message to her brothers, letting them know where she was working. After Christmas she had a letter from them telling her that at last Hamish had been married. The letter went on to complain bitterly about her leaving the farm. They had got a girl in to do the housework, but she was no good, no good at all. Oh well, thought Fanny, things would be better now. Hamish's wife would be able to take over the management of the household.

It was a long severe winter. Fanny saw the children through colds and then in turn through the measles. But at last the winter broke up and April arrived, with the grass turning green and the buds showing on the trees.

It was towards the middle of April that she got another letter from her brothers. This letter was very peremptory. Fanny must come home at once. Hamish's wife, Mabel, was finding the work too much for her. She couldn't manage the stove (Fanny smiled grimly as she remembered the old stove) and she found that the churning troubled her back. With spring coming on the work would increase, and — well, there was nothing for it. Fanny must come home.

Fanny had no intention of going home, but she showed the letter to Mrs. Van Buskirk.

"Oh Fanny! " wailed that lady pathetically, "you can't leave me now. How would I ever get on without you? Who would look after me? And who would care for my poor dear children? "

When Fanny showed the letter to the doctor, he said in his gruff way, "No, no. It's impossible. My office — my patients. You're indispensable. We can't let you go."

And he raised her wages three dollars a month.

As Fanny sat on the edge of her bed that night, writing a letter to her brothers, she suddenly put the pen back in the inkpot and began to laugh. All her life she had been at the beck and call of other people. But tonight she felt a new hope, a new stirring of self-confidence. Here were two groups of people, her brothers and the Van Buskirks, both of whom felt that they could not possibly get on without her. It dawned on her that she had it in her power to impress her will on others for a change. How she would do it she did not know. But she went to sleep confident that somehow she would let the world know that she was a person to be reckoned with, not just a convenience without human rights.

Next morning, on the strength of her new assurance, she took some of the money she had saved and bought herself a new dress and a new hat. She was particularly pleased with the hat. It was not just a bonnet, but a real hat, and it was trimmed with pretty ribbons and a small bunch of flowers.

When she went to church the following Sunday, people who had never before recognized her, took occasion to bow to her and wish her a good day. And after the service the minister, a big sandy-haired Scot who stuttered, took her hand in both of his and said, "It d-d-does a man's heart g-g-good to see you, Miss McClintock. You look as young and fresh as a spring m-m-morning."

She knew that he was exaggerating. It takes more than a spring hat to smooth the wrinkles out of a woman's forehead. But she was pleased. Never before had anyone complimented her on her appearance.

On a morning in June she heard a timid knock on the back door, and when she opened it she saw her brother John standing there. He was wearing his best tweed suit and on his gnarled face was an ingratiating smile.

"Hello Fanny," he said.

"Come in John," said Fanny.

He came in and deposited his large frame on a kitchen chair. For some minutes he sat there saying nothing. It was obvious that he was undergoing a struggle. He had removed his big straw hat and he kept nervously moving it from one knee to the other.

Fanny knew what was going on in his mind. He wanted to beg her to return to the farm, but he was finding it hard to knuckle under to a woman.

"Yes John? " Fanny said finally.

"You've got to come home."

"I'm perfectly contented here, John."

"It's like this, Fanny. Mabel — I don't like to speak ill of my brother's wife — but she can't manage at all."

"She will learn, John."

"You don't know what we have to put up with, Fanny. Her pies — the upper crust is burned to a cinder, while the lower crust is raw dough. And stew — she gives us stew six times a week, and always scorched."

"Yes John. That old stove was always hard to manage."

"But don't you see, Fanny — what will we do when the harvesters come? They won't put up with that sort of thing."

"Very true, John. They used to like my cooking, didn't they? "

Fanny smiled contentedly and brushed a wisp of hair out of her eyes.

"Then you'll come, Fanny? " His tone was eager and his eyes pleaded with her humbly.

"They pay me good wages here."

"Wages? "

"Yes John. Wages."

He blinked in perplexity. What could the woman be driving at?

"You don't mean, Fanny, that you would expect us to pay you wages? "

"I do that, John. Mind you, I'm not saying that I have any intention of going back. But if I do I'll expect twenty dollars a month."

"Losh woman" said John aghast at her presumption. "What would you be doing with all that money? "

"I'd be buying myself some clothes and such like odds and ends. You'd be surprised, John, what a woman can do with a little money."

"Whoever heard of a man paying wages to his sister? "

"You're hearing of it now, John. And that stove — "

"Well," he conceded grudgingly, "we might manage to pick up a good second-hand stove."

"Not second-hand, John. I want a new stove with a tank for hot water at one end and a warming oven above."

"But," he protested, "we couldn't afford a stove like that. Such a stove would cost a terrible lot of money."

"You're forgetting that I know what father left you in his will. You can afford that and more. That parlor now."

"What's wrong with the parlor? It does fine for Duncan and his handiwork."

"Duncan can take his handiwork elsewhere. I want the parlor for company."

"What company? "

"It would be real nice to entertain some of the neighbors in the parlor."

"You meet the neighbors at the church, and they rally round at harvest time. What more do you want? "

"I want to entertain them in the parlor. Now, that old furniture — it's falling to pieces."

"Duncan can fix it up with a touch of glue."

"You know very well it's too late for that. The wood's all dry and brittle.

"If we were entertaining the minister and his wife — the minister's a heavy man. You wouldn't want the chair to collapse under him, now would you, John? "

"The minister can sit in the kitchen as he has always done."

"Not any longer. If I'm going back — mind you, I haven't said that I'm willing to go. They're very good to me here and I like it fine. But if I do go back, I want to have things real nice and comfortable for a change."

"Fanny, Fanny," he said sorrowfully, "you're a hard woman."

"I have hard men to deal with, John."

Poor man! He squirmed, protested and argued. But it was to no avail. Fanny had him by the throat and he knew it. Before he went off down the lane, muttering to himself, he had agreed unconditionally to all her terms.

Fanny gave notice to the Van Buskirks and left at the end of the month. When she arrived at the farm she was greeted by her brothers and her sister-in-law as if she were returning from a long journey. Her sister-in-law was a sweet little woman whose father was storekeeper in a nearby village. She was willing enough to work, but she was quite incapable of doing everything that was expected of a woman on a farm. She was very glad to hand over the management of affairs to Fanny.

Fanny for her part set about putting things to rights in no time. She got her new stove immediately, and when the harvesting was over and the fall plowing was done, she got after the men to start re-decorating and re-furnishing the parlor. If they demurred at the expense, she had a scheme that always made them toe the line. She would pack her bag, put on her bonnet, and sit on the back porch as if waiting to be called for. It worked every time. She got everything she wanted — fresh wallpaper in the parlor, a new carpet on the floor, and fine new furniture, including a sofa upholstered with a pretty flowered tapestry. She also insisted on a coal stove to sit in the middle of the parlor floor.

By the time everything was ready — including a set of china dishes for company — Christmas had arrived. Fanny entertained Mabel's family for Christmas dinner, and after dinner they all sat in the parlor exchanging gossip and telling yarns. She next entertained the minister and his wife, and finally some of the neighbors for a game of euchre.

In the end her brothers came to enjoy the new way of life, and would themselves suggest that they have a few friends in for a game of cards. And the guests never failed to arrive, no matter how inclement the weather. It was mighty cosy on a cold winter night, with the wind howling about the eaves, to sit around a glowing coal fire making hearts trump, or playing it alone, or slamming your right bower on your opponent's ace.

And then there was always Fanny's midnight supper to look forward to — cold chicken and cold ham with potato salad, pickles and jam or jelly. And of course Fanny's pies, raspberry, currant, or apple.

Fanny continued to work from daylight to dark. She would not have been happy to do otherwise. But this was now her house, and she dominated it as had her father before her.

GOOD-BYE TO AN AGE
by Dora Macdonald, Helen Ball,
and Norman McPherson

At the time of the Boer War, Canada was in its awkward adolescence. We were not sure of ourselves. Sometimes our behavior was reasonably adult, sometimes it was pathetically immature, but always it was excessively emotional. As a nation we were groping for an identity. We were still a dependency of Great Britain, a bright jewel in Queen Victoria's imperial crown. But there were stirrings of independence. Laurier, who was very much the imperialist, sent a contingent of two thousand troops to South Africa. But Bourassa in Quebec protested. He felt that Laurier was setting a bad precedent by aiding Britain in one of her foreign wars. But in Ontario we were thoroughly British. Our patriotism was unthinking and exuberant. As so often happens when surging emotions control human beings, we often made supreme fools of ourselves.

Our participation in the war provided a marvelous opportunity for would-be poets to spout. I remember the chorus of one of the songs we sang:

> "Though our homes are far from the motherland,
>   We're British none the less, sir;
>   And ready, aye ready, to fight and die,
>   For our flag and Queen, God bless her."

I have forgotten the verses, but they were the same kind of fulsome drivel. It makes us ashamed now to think that we could ever give voice to such phoney heroics. We gloried in the fact that we could fight for the mother country:

Canada to the Mother Country

I have bade good-bye to my boys, mother,
With an aching pain at my heart;
And have wept that the sea, that has borne them from me,
May forever keep us apart.

Brave lads how they struggled to smile, mother,
As we locked in a last embrace;
But I knew ere the ships had quitted the slips,
There were tears on each manly face.

My boys will not flinch nor fail, mother,
You may send them back wearied and worn;
But they'd rather be dead than hanging their head,
And they'd rather have scars than scorn.

And then the final stanza:

You'll be kind for my sake to the lads, mother,
And you'll pray for their lives to God;
And if any return not to their homes again,
When they fall on the field they will fall like men,
On a British African sod.

In an obscure corner of the archives in Ottawa there is a despatch which reveals, sad to relate, that when the raw Canadian troups first came under fire they did "flinch and fail". But believe me, they later fully redeemed themselves, especially at Paardeburg.

Though I was only eleven at the time I knew that those verses were mawkish doggerel. Why I memorized them I don't remember. But that is the sort of emotionalism we indulged in during the South African War. When General White and his small command were besieged in Ladysmith, we were overwrought with anxiety, and we followed the progress of the relief army under General Buller with avid eagerness.

In church one morning Mr. Farthing, our rector (later Bishop Farthing) interrupted the service to announce in sepulchral tones, "General White is cutting his way out of Ladysmith." In my childish imagination I saw General White and his soldiers slashing about vainly with their swords as they staggered and died.

At a patriotic concert a very stout woman (she had been handsome in her youth, but was now much overblown) had somehow got hold of a military uniform. She bulged it out in all directions, but she recited with patriotic fervor Kipling's ballad

"Pass the hat for your credit's sake, and pay, pay, pay."

Two teachers on the high school staff tried to tell us the Boer's side of the story, but they were immediately labelled pro-Boer, and they almost got themselves fired.

Ladysmith was ultimately relieved on March 1, 1900. There had been a belated very heavy snowfall, and I lost a valued bracelet in a snowbank. But I remember vividly the riotous celebration, with marching bands, patriotic speeches, and bonfires in the streets.

"So the dear old lady is gone." It is my mother's voice I hear and its sadness has lingered for more than seventy years. There were tears in her eyes as she took me on her knee and told me about the good queen who had lived in a palace away across the ocean in England. And now she was dead.

To me, not yet five years old, the word "dead" meant being buried in the garden like Tommy, our pet cat who recently had died. But mother assured me that Queen Victoria was already safely in Heaven.

That seemed to comfort both of us but I still remember with a sense of sadness, watching mother sew a black crepe band on the sleeve of my father's overcoat; still remember letters of condolence being written on black edged note paper to our relatives in England; still remember the Union Jack flying at half mast on Jesse Ketchum school and Yorkville town hall.

And I'm sure many a black velvet hat was divested of a bright quill or posy. Mother and the aunts would not have considered attending a memorial service for "our dear queen" in anything but solemn and severe black. I remember the feeling of blackness in church. Toronto was draped in it for weeks.

When I was seven, our grandparents who lived next door, moved away and their old accumulated magazines, among which were several copies of the illustrated London News, found their way into our house. My brothers (aged eight and twelve) and I lay on our stomachs on the carpeted livingroom floor (family-room today) and devoured them, particularly the one given over to stories and pictures of Queen Victoria's funeral, all of which after more than two years was still dinner table conversation.

We were a sailing family, interested in boats of any sort and very navy conscious. We children owned the British navy, from tenders to battle ships; stamped out of heavy cardboard and mounted on small blocks of wood. Imagine how thrilled we were with the story of the navy tender, Alberta, bearing the Queen's body, her bier draped in ruby velvet, white satin embroidered in gold, and finally the royal standard, crossing the Solent and passing through the great fleet the Queen herself had been so proud to call her own.

The royal family followed in the royal yacht, Victoria and Albert. From Gosport, where they docked, the bier was taken by special train to Victoria Station, London. There was much in the account about the lying in state, the funeral procession and the many royal dignitaries who came from abroad to pay their last respects. But it was the navy bit that fascinated us.

While verifying some of the above material, I found some interesting facts about the twenty-fourth of May. To us children it was firecracker day — a day of excitement and fun.

The twenty-fourth of May
Is the Queen's birthday
If you don't give us a holiday
We'll all run away.

But our threat was needless because the queen's birthday was named Victoria Day by the legislature of the United Canadas in 1845 and 1901 the Canadian Parliament proclaimed it a national holiday. In 1898 patriotic fervor prompted the proposal of an Empire Day on which appropriate exercises would be carried out in the schools. The day before the queen's birthday was chosen as suitable, so EMPIRE DAY was first observed on May 23, 1899. In my school days it meant solemn speeches, songs, cadet parades and much waving of Union Jacks, all in honour of the British Empire and the great queen who had reigned for sixty-three years.

The pomp and glory of her reign has slipped back into history, but many Toronto citizens still recall the sense of loss and the long period of mourning, official and otherwise, that followed the death of Victoria Regina, at Cowes on the Isle of Wight, on February 5, 1901.

* * *

"Mother, Daddy, Uncle, come quick! Something has happened to the sky."

I was only seven years old but, looking south from my bedroom window, I knew the sky should be dusk-grey, not bright orange-pink.

My urgent summons brought all three on the run and up went the window, letting in the hubbub and strident clang of the fire reels leaving our local fire hall. We stood there listening and presently heard the fainter clang of more reels from other parts of the city. Toronto was a quiet city in those days, particularly at night, and that ominous clanging still rings in my memory accompanied by a shiver of excitement and fear. Were we in danger?

It was April 19, 1904. Telephones were still a luxury. We did not have one but in no time flat, my father and my uncle were off and away on their bicycles, while Mother, saying "God will look after us, dear" pulled down the blind and tucked me back into bed.

Our house was on Collier Street, two blocks above Bloor near Park Road and, as we learned later, nearly two miles from the fire. When the blaze was at its fiercest, smoking embers fell as far away as College Street in spite of a brisk north wind.

The first alarm came at 8.04 in the evening from someone who noticed smoke issuing from a building on Wellington Street between Bay and Yonge. The fire department responded on the double. In record time hoses were trained on the burning building from third floor windows of the building next door.

But suddenly the lower floor of that building was blazing and the firemen were trapped. They escaped by sliding down their hoses only minutes before the whole structure was enveloped in flames and the roof fell in.

With the wind doing its wicked best, flames leaped from building to building and before long the fire was out of control on both sides of Bay below Wellington. Hamilton, London, Buffalo and Peterborough responded to calls for help by sending firemen and equipment on special trains that, hopefully, were given a clear run to Toronto.

Who doesn't stop and watch with a sense of excitement if he happens to be near a fire station (we called them fire halls) when today's huge motorized vehicles come snorting out with their sirens screaming? For me the memory of a clanging bell and a matched team of greys hauling an old fashioned hook 'n' ladder has even a greater thrill. The horses were stalled with their harness hanging above them and their response to an alarm was as keen and efficient as the response of the men who handled them and got the fire fighting equipment on its way in a matter of minutes.

The old fire engine (a steam driven pump) with its attendant fireman and engineer, was a heavy cumbersome machine needing three horses abreast to haul it. A special horse-drawn wagon kept it supplied with coal. Strategically positioned "steamers" controlled the water pressure in the hoses.

Picture this 1904 equipment, the horses and the sweating firemen in the light of dozens of flaming buildings. Picture, too, the upturned faces of onlookers. Thousands watched for hours. Fortunately there was no loss of life but fourteen acres of smoking ruins greeted Torontonians the next morning.

Yes, the night of the great fire stays with me. On toward morning I woke to hear voices and the clink of teacups coming from the kitchen. The uncarpeted back stairs were cold to my bare feet but Daddy would put his arms around me and tell me the danger was past.

He did. Two days later he took me to see the ruins — blackened crumbling walls standing like old sad monuments and heaps of indescribable rubble with wisps of smoke still rising as if in supplication.

When Sir Wilfred Laurier, after fifteen years as Prime Minister, was decisively beaten in the critical election of 1911, he wrote, "It is becoming more and more manifest to me that it was not reciprocity that was turned down but a Catholic premier."

Nothing could be further from the truth. There will always be some people so opposed to Catholicism that they will vote against any Catholic politician no matter how meritorious he may be. But at that time their number was few, and their influence was cancelled by those staunch Catholics who would always vote for a Catholic politician merely because he was a Catholic. The great majority of Canadians regarded Laurier as a charming and cultured gentleman, whose religion was his own business.

No. It was not anti-Catholicism that defeated Laurier. It was our staunch loyalty to the Empire and our aggressive Canadianism.

When Laurier's finance minister introduced into parliament the reciprocity agreement, which called for either the reduction or the abolition of all tariffs on goods traded between Canada and the United States, the Conservative party leaders were thoroughly dejected. They felt that it would be quite useless to fight such a policy in the forthcoming election on economic grounds. And with considerable cynicism they decided to appeal to our patriotic sentiments and our fear of being absorbed into the United States. Legend, with what truth I do not know, attributes to Stephen Leacock the idea of using "no truck or trade with the Yankees" as the battle cry in the election campaign. As Bruce Hutchison in his book "Mr. Prime Minister" points out, President Taft, jolly and impulsive Taft, played into the Conservatives' hands when he declared that Canada had reached "The parting of the ways". Nor did Champ Clark, the speaker of the House of Representatives, help matters when he announced that "we are prepared to annex Canada."

In the election campaign the Liberals argued with convincing logic that the reciprocity agreement would be for the economic good of Canada, would put money in our pockets. But we responded with unselfish patriotic fervor, "Damn the ten cents. We stand for the British Empire." And the majority of us cast our votes against Laurier, and for the Conservative party.

If Laurier had won the election and the agreement had been signed, what would have been the result? One wonders. Would Canada have remained in the main a seller of natural products, and a buyer of manufactured goods? Or would she have gone on to a fuller and richer economic development?

* * *

On the morning of April 15th, in the year 1912, I was travelling on the train from Kingston to London, when I was startled by the cry of a newsboy, who had picked up a bundle of Toronto newspapers at one of the way stations. I could scarcely believe my ears. What the boy was calling out was incredible, fantastic. A shiver of alarm went through the whole coach.

The Titanic, the most modern, the most luxurious liner ever built, had struck an iceberg on her maiden voyage and was calling for help. The news of the shocking accident was meagre. But it appeared that there would be little loss of life. The magnificent vessel was still afloat, and every ship in her vicinity was rushing to her assistance.

As the day wore on (it was a Monday) special editions of many newspapers were published. But the additional news consisted mostly of rumors and surmises, or contradictory statements, until the evening papers came out with a report that made everyone breathe more freely. The great ship was still afloat, and was being towed into Halifax harbor. All the passengers had been transferred to the liners Carpathia and Parisian. Everyone said, with a sigh of relief, "Of course, that is what would happen. Isn't she the marvelous new unsinkable ship? "

But by morning the appalling truth began to leak out of the White Star office in New-York. There had been a major disaster at sea, how great a disaster nobody as yet knew. It was several days before the general public was informed of what had really happened.

When the Titanic was being built, reports of her fascinating construction were issued regularly to the press. She was to be the pride of the ocean, a floating palace, a marvel of technological and scientific achievement, the symbol of our age's astounding progress. With a double bottom and sixteen watertight compartments, she was to be, we were told, the first truly unsinkable ship. To be sure, watertight compartments had already been installed in several ships, and as Benjamin Franklin had pointed out, the Chinese had been using the idea for generations in their junks. But never before had the plan been adopted so extensively in building a big passenger liner. Even if the Titanic did meet with some mishap, she was equipped with that other scientific marvel, radio, to enable her to call for help. The last word in naval construction, she was to open the way to eliminating the danger of any large scale tragedy at sea.

The shock to our pride when she proved to be as fragile as a cockle shell when she encountered an iceberg, still reverberates in our minds today. Of her 2,000 passengers, less than a third were rescued from the sea and brought into New York by the Carpathia.

The following year (that is in 1913) there occurred what has ever since been known as the Great Storm. It was the worst storm that ever took place on the Great Lakes. It lasted from November 7 to November 12 For six days the terrific winds lashed the waters of the lakes, especially Lake Huron, into a tumult of surging breakers. The waves came, not as on the Atlantic where they succeed each other at regular intervals, but one on the back of the other, so that three might waves would crash into a ship before she had time to right herself after the previous onslaught. Often the wind gusted to over 80 miles an hour, and with the wind came driving snow or rain that reduced visibility to zero. To weather the storm all ships would naturally head into the gale, but many of them, even with their engines going full out, could not maintain this position, and were battered into the trough of the waves, where they rolled helplessly.

Thirty-nine vessels, all of them sizable lake freighters, were wrecked. Twenty of these ships were stranded on the shore, eleven were completely destroyed, and eight vanished without trace, presumably capsized or battered to pieces by the fury of the waves. Two hundred and forty-eight sailors lost their lives. Fortunately all the big passenger boats had been laid up for the season, or the loss of life would have been much higher.

Even on shore the destruction was appalling. Trees were uprooted, chimneys were blown down, roofs were torn off, and all means of travel and communication were disrupted. Telephone and telegraph wires were down; and trains, delayed by the driving snow and rain, were quite unable to maintain even the semblance of a schedule.

* * *

These two disasters seemed to forecast a greater disaster to follow. On June 28, 1914, the Archduke Franz Ferdinand of Austria-Hungary, was shot at Sarajevo, an obscure village in Serbia. We, reading about the incident in the papers, wondered how in hell to pronounce Sarajevo (we later learned how to pronounce many strange foreign names) and shrugged the matter off as of no concern to us. It was just another of those tiresome things that were always happening in the turbulent middle-European countries. It was summer, and summer in Canada is a glorious season. Some of us were at our summer cottages, some were sailing on the Great Lakes, some were just lolling in hammocks in our own back yards. None of us had any idea of what was going on in the chancellories of Europe. Even as July dreamed its way into history we failed to hear in our imaginations the ominous rattle of gun-carriages on the move, and the thud of marching feet.

Robert Borden, the prime minister, was resting at a resort hotel in Muskoka. He remained there, quite unaware of the storm clouds that were forming in Europe, until his secretary summoned him back to Ottawa five days before war broke out. The general public knew nothing of his hurried return to the capital, or of the feverish days that followed.

When the headlines in our newspapers screamed that Britain was at war with Germany, we were stunned, incredulous, bewildered. The glorious days of our carefree youth were vanishing. The winds of change were sweeping us into an unknown future. Our cherished dream of security and progress had burst like an irridescent bubble. Our golden age was becoming just a few forgotten pages in the annals of our country, and a new and very different age was looming above the horizon.